W9-BCU-810

POLITICAL CAMPAIGNING

POLITICAL CAMPAIGNING

Problems in Creating an Informed Electorate

By

STANLEY KELLEY, JR.

THE BROOKINGS INSTITUTION

WASHINGTON, D. C.

THE BROOKINGS INSTITUTION is an independent organization engaged in research and education in the social sciences. Its principal purposes are to aid in the development of sound public policies and to provide advanced training for students in the social sciences.

The Institution was founded December 8, 1927, as a consolidation of three antecedent organizations: the Institute for Government Research, 1916; the Institute of Economics, 1922; and the Robert Brookings Graduate School of Economics and Government, 1924.

The general administration of the Institution is the responsibility of a self-perpetuating Board of Trustees. In addition to this general responsibility the By-Laws provide that, "It is the function of the Trustees to make possible the conduct of scientific research and publication, under the most favorable conditions, and to safeguard the independence of the research staff in the pursuit of their studies and in the publication of the results of such studies. It is not a part of their function to determine, control, or influence the conduct of particular investigations or the conclusions reached." The immediate direction of the policies, program, and staff of the Institution is vested in the President, who is assisted by an advisory council, chosen from the professional staff of the Institution.

In publishing a study, the Institution presents it as a competent treatment of a subject worthy of public consideration. The interpretations and conclusions in such publications are those of the author or authors and do not necessarily reflect the views of other members of the Brookings staff or of the administrative officers of the Institution.

Foreword

THIS BOOK EXAMINES a series of contemporary campaign practices, advances suggestions for their reform, and shows how they affect the ability of voters to make informed choices at the polls. The author's careful delineation of standards for evaluating campaign discussion, the information he marshals in considering the problems of public policy suggested by his analysis, and his review of attempts to deal with those problems make a substantial contribution to an understanding of the strengths and weaknesses of the campaign as a political institution. His work may also lead to a re-thinking of some of the explanations of campaign behavior current in the literature.

The book grew out of Mr. Kelley's previous study of public relations techniques in politics, which he prepared for publication while a Brookings Research Fellow in 1955-56, and which was published under the title *Professional Public Relations and Political Power* by the Johns Hopkins Press in 1956. It is also closely related to, and was influenced by, two other studies undertaken by the Institution's Governmental Studies Division, *Television and Presidential Politics* (1956) by Charles A. H. Thomson and *The Politics of National Party Conventions* (1960) by Paul T. David, Ralph M. Goldman, and Richard C. Bain. With the latter it is a part of a series of election year studies of party institutions and party electoral and nominating activities that also includes Richard C. Bain's *Decisions and Voting Records of National Party Conventions,* Ralph M. Goldman's *Trends in National Party Leadership,* and *The Presidential Campaign and Election of 1956* by Charles A. H. Thomson and Frances M. Shattuck.

The Institution and the author are grateful to the members of the committee who reviewed and criticized the manuscript in its final stages. These included George A. Graham, Paul T. David, and Walter S. Salant, of the Brookings staff; Charles A. H. Thomson of the Rand Corporation; Wallace Carroll of the *New York Times* Washington Bureau; and Carl B. Swisher of the Johns Hopkins University. The Institution and the author are also indebted to others who have read and criticized the manuscript and who have made many valuable suggestions for its improvement: S. T. Beza, Harwood L. Childs, Walter F. Murphy, and Sidney Verba, all of Princeton University; Albert Roland of the United States Information Agency; Laurin L. Henry of the Brookings Institution; Bruce L. Felknor of the Fair Campaign Practices Committee; and Richard C. Bain and Sidney Reiss. The book was edited by A. Evelyn Breck and indexed by Marcia T. Marple.

The Institution is indebted to the Ford Foundation for financial support that has made this study possible. The conclusions and recommendations are those of the author and were reached wholly independently of the Ford Foundation, which should not be understood as approving or disapproving the views expressed herein.

ROBERT D. CALKINS
President

June 1960

Contents

POLITICAL CAMPAIGNING

Chapter V

Chapter VI

Chapter VII

Chapter VIII

1

Introduction

THE CHARACTER OF political campaigns in the United States has been a continuing source of dissatisfaction to friendly students of American political life. At the turn of the century indignation with current electioneering and campaign methods was an important feature of reform movements. The long list of proscribed practices written into state election codes at that time—including vote buying, treating, bribery of editors, repeat voting, and intimidation—record some of the least savory tactics used by campaigners as well as the success of reformers in arousing the public. Woodrow Wilson put the issue as the reformers saw it—a choice between "government by control" and "government by discussion."[1] He did not define these phrases, but his meaning was clear: The public business should be carried on in the full view of the public. The politician should owe his office to his ability to persuade an informed electorate of his qualifications for office and of the wisdom of his policies, and to that ability alone. He should not be able to win and maintain power because he could buy or manufacture votes, or because the public was ignorant of his activities.

Since Wilson's time, the campaign practices that most obviously frustrate government by discussion have been disappearing. Political machines have declined in strength;

[1] John Wells Davidson, *A Crossroads of Freedom: The 1912 Campaign Speeches of Woodrow Wilson* (1956), p. 454.

1

fraud has been brought under more or less effective control. Partly for this reason, partly because the growth of the mass media of communication has provided the technical basis for large-scale propaganda efforts, recent critics of campaign tactics increasingly have emphasized another persistent, and more troubling, theme of American political commentary: that the discussion found in campaigns tends to impair the judgment of the electorate and to upset the formulation of coherent public policies.[2] Evidence tendered for this conclusion includes the normal occurrence in campaign advertising and speeches of excessive and sentimental concern with personality, appeals to prejudice and irrationality, libelous accusations, gross distortions of fact, promises not to be fulfilled, and evasiveness and ambiguity in the presentation of a meager offering of issues. The Wilsonian ideal receives a sharper scrutiny, it would seem, the more closely it is approached.

A number of important issues are raised in and by this criticism of campaign discussion. Is it justified, and, if so, on what grounds? How prevalent are the features of campaign discussion that the critics condemn? In what circumstances do they occur? What, if anything, can be done about them? The

[2] To cite a few examples: see James Reston, "Our Campaign Techniques Reexamined," *New York Times Magazine* (Nov. 9, 1952), p. 8; William Lee Miller, "Can Government be 'Merchandized'?" *The Reporter* (Oct. 27, 1953), pp. 11-16; and Walter Lippmann, *Essays in the Public Philosophy* (1956), pp. 27-29. Madison, Tocqueville, Bryce, and Ostrogorski are among the classical commentators on American politics who have been either distrustful or disdainful of most campaign discussion. Ostrogorski held, for example, that "when the average man descends into the arena of public life, at election time, he is—he who is so intelligent and so clever in practical life—like a Samson shorn of his strength; and the Philistines of the party Organization have an easy task when they undertake to provide his 'political education' offhand, in view of the vote which they want to snatch from him. To the elector, whose food during the years which intervene between elections has been confined to the opium of the party newspapers, they administer a stronger dose of it." M. Ostrogorski, *Democracy and the Organization of Political Parties* (1902), Vol. II, p. 327.

2

purpose of the present study is to give at least partial answers to these questions.

Whether or not one considers any body of criticism as justifiable depends in part, of course, on the standards of value one regards as applicable to a given state of affairs. This simple observation is appropriate here, because students of politics at the present time are not very certain about the standards they should use for evaluating campaign discussion. Efforts to explore the social implications of campaigning have been far less frequent than descriptions of its strategies, tactics, and immediate effects. As a result, we can specify in some detail what a campaigner would lose if he should disarm unilaterally but have little to say about what society would gain or lose if all parties to campaigns should declare a truce. So long as this lack of agreement on the social objectives to be realized in campaigns persists, there will also be lack of agreement on the validity of any particular criticism of campaigns as they are.

This study will attempt to show, however, that much of the dissatisfaction with the character of our campaigns is eminently justified if one basic assumption is granted: that campaign discussion should help voters make rational voting decisions. If the rational voting decision is defined carefully, the features of a campaign discussion that will contribute to such a decision can be deduced from the definition itself, from some simple assumptions about the psychology of voters, and from the basic character of the campaign situation. Such a procedure yields the elements of a model campaign discussion against which campaign discussion as it actually occurs can be measured systematically and objectively.

When this is done, it becomes quite clear that contemporary campaign discussion falls far short of meeting a number of the requirements of a discussion that would encourage rational voting, for the critics have thoroughly documented

3

the existence of particular abuses. It is obvious, for instance, that campaign discussion projects a highly distorted view of the choices the voter faces and a closer examination reveals a patterned quality in these distortions. It is obvious also that certain practices that tend to subvert rationality in voting—libelous attacks on candidates or mis-identification of the sources of campaign propaganda, to cite two examples—occur often enough to warrant concern. While in other instances it is not always possible to show conclusively that what is a possible problem is also an actual one, available data do give some indication of whether or not this is true.

It is the conclusion of this study that something can be done about the shortcomings of campaign discussion: that it can be made to take forms that will contribute to greater rationality in voting. This is contrary to the conclusion, and even more to the tone, of much of the literature on campaigning. Many of those interested in the realistic analysis of politics have held that the differences between campaign discussion in the real world and a discussion that would contribute to rational electoral action are inherent in the very nature of the campaign situation. The arguments offered to support this contention are persuasive enough to have made the author feel, more than once, that specifying the features of a rational campaign discourse might be a utopian enterprise. While the most convincing response to arguments that nothing can be done is to show what can be, it may be worthwhile to indicate briefly the point at which the "realist" analysis becomes misleading.

Basically, the realists have argued that the shortcomings of campaign discussion are the inevitable products of the strategies campaigners find it necessary to adopt in the struggle for votes. This argument is, on the whole, a valid one. By leaving the matter here, however, the realists have invited the inference that the particular strategies that produce these shortcomings are also inevitable. The case for

4

this proposition is much less solid. Strategy is strictly relative to situation, and some of the characteristic strategies found in American campaigns are a response to conditions that are subject to change. By altering some of these conditions, a brand of campaign discussion that will encourage rational voting can be made to be in the interests of campaigners as well as of voters.

The principal tasks undertaken in the present study should be clear from what has been said this far: It seeks to define standards for evaluating campaign discussion, to identify deviations from these standards in contemporary campaign discussion, to examine the causes of these deviations, and to prescribe measures that will help to reduce them. Something must now be said about its limitations.

First, it deals with what is really only one part of the discussion process in campaigns. Any political campaign can be usefully thought of as involving at least four sub-campaigns: A money raising campaign, a campaign for the support of party leaders, a campaign for the support of interest group leaders, and a public campaign directed to the electorate at large. Discussion and persuasion play an important role in all of these campaigns, but it is only discussion in the last of these that will be examined here.

Secondly, unless otherwise indicated, the term "campaign" as it will be used here refers to the general election campaigns of candidates for public office. Obviously, the discussion of policies, personalities, and issues that goes on in the period between the nomination and election of candidates is only one phase in campaigning and in the discussion process that attends governmental action. Many of the observations that can be made about it would seem to apply equally well to campaigning in primaries and to political discussion between campaigns, but this study will make such applications only occasionally.

Thirdly, certain features of the environment in which

American campaigns occur are taken as given in this study, a fact that limits the kinds of reform proposals it considers. Among these are a government of separated powers and federal structure, a two party system with relatively undisciplined parties, elections based on fixed terms of office in single member districts, and the constitutional protection of the freedoms of speech and press. Although all of these features of American political life have a profound effect on the character of discussion in campaigns, only those proposals for action that do not presuppose abandoning them will be dealt with.

Fourthly, the standards for evaluating campaign discussion adopted in this study are not the only ones that could be adopted, or that deserve consideration. Walter Lippmann has argued, for instance, that campaigns and elections are substitutes for violence in the settlement of community disputes;[3] and Pendleton Herring has praised them for helping build a general acquiescence in the actions of government and an inclusive sense of responsibility for them.[4] Both views suggest valid alternative (though not necessarily conflicting) approaches to measuring the value of campaign discussion.

Finally, this study makes no effort to go behind its major premise that rationality in voting is desirable. There have been very few who have argued that the irrationality of voters is beneficial in a democracy; and the arguments of these few are not very convincing. Nevertheless, the premise is open to question on philosophical grounds. It is conceivable also that greater rationality in voting might have some unforeseen consequences that the democrat would find undesirable. Certainly the issue is not a closed one.

[3] See *The Phantom Public* (1925), p. 58.
[4] See *The Politics of Democracy* (1940), p. 257. *Cf.* W. J. M. Mackenzie, who suggests that elections "commit the people to a sense of responsibility for their own betterment more effectively than any form of exhortation yet devised by Ministries of Propaganda or of Information." "The Export of Electoral Systems," *Political Studies* (October 1957), p. 255.

This much should suffice to introduce succeeding chapters. Chapter 2 attempts to specify the kind of campaign discussion that can contribute to rationality in voting and to show that the realization of this kind of discussion is at least theoretically possible. Chapters 3-7 are "how to" chapters. They examine how to realize or approximate the various features of a campaign discussion that would contribute to electoral rationality. In so doing, they examine also both the shortcomings of contemporary campaign discussion and the sources of these shortcomings. Chapter 3 discusses the problems involved in ensuring the kind of audience exposure to campaign discussion that rationality in voting presupposes. Chapter 4 seeks to show how distortion, ambiguity, and irrelevancy in campaign discussion might be reduced. Chapters 5 and 6 examine the difficulties involved in controlling unfair personal attacks on candidates and some measures that would help to overcome such difficulties. Chapter 7 discusses how mis-identification of the sources of campaign propaganda may impair rationality in voting and what might be done about it. Chapter 8 is a general summary.

2

The Informing Function

A SET OF STANDARDS for evaluating campaign discussion is
logically prior to useful criticism of it or suggestions for re-
forming it. The somewhat pedestrian purpose of the present
chapter is to make clear the standards that will be applied in
this study and to defend them as realistic. It will also seek to
show their similarity to, and departures from, those adopted
by other students or critics of campaigning.

In defining any set of standards for evaluating campaign
discussion, one must answer two questions: What is the
purpose of such discussion? What must it be like to serve
this purpose? The answer the present study gives to the first
of these questions has already been indicated: Campaign discussion should help voters make rational voting decisions. It
has an informing function.

This conception of the purpose of campaigning is in no
way novel, for the belief that campaigners should educate
and inform the public underlies most of the critical comment on campaign discussion. It might be termed the official
view of what campaigns mean—the one taken by the courts,
taught in the schools, and offered by politicians on public
occasions. Justice Wiley Rutledge expressed it in a fairly
typical way when he wrote that the fullest exercise of the
rights of free speech and assembly "is essential to the full,
fair, and untrammeled operation of the electoral system. To
the extent they are curtailed, the electorate is deprived of in-

formation, knowledge, and opinion vital to its function."[1] James A. Woodburn was adopting this view also when he called the campaign a "vast school of instruction" and praised it as an occasion on which "people heed instruction from the platform and press who take but little interest in public discussion at other times."[2]

The definition of the purposes of campaign discussion given above, however, specifies the educational objectives of campaign discussion somewhat more clearly than statements like those of Rutledge or Woodburn. Such clarity is important if we are to be able to determine whether or not campaigns "educate." To say that campaigns should encourage rational voting carries no implication, as does Woodburn's statement, that campaigners are to further the general political education of the electorate. It does imply what Rutledge never says in so many words, that information, knowledge, and opinion are vital to the electorate because voters need them to make rational decisions at the polls. The extent to which rationality in voting is encouraged thus becomes the measure of the value of discussion in campaigns.

Rational Voting

To make "rationality in voting" a usable measure, of course, requires giving the term a precise meaning; otherwise we shall have exchanged the ambiguity involved in the word "education" for that involved in the word "rationality." As the term will be used here, full rationality in voting would require full information about the alternatives to be voted

[1] *United States* v. *Congress of Industrial Organizations et al.*, 335 U.S. 106 (1948).
[2] *Political Parties and Party Problems in the United States* (1903), pp. 205-06.

9

upon, full knowledge of all the effects that would attend the choice of each alternative, and a comprehensive and logically consistent system of preferences, within which values may be assigned to each of these effects.[3]

To state it another way, the voter would have to know what it is that distinguishes the candidates for a particular office, one from another; and he would need sufficient information to predict the future consequences of these differences for the realization of the purposes he holds to be most important. If he did possess such information, and if his set of values were comprehensive and logically consistent, new arguments would have nothing further to contribute to the rightness (from his own point of view) of his choice.

While the bare statement of such a conception of rationality in voting is enough to indicate that it must be imperfectly realized in practice, defining it in this manner helps make clear what would be involved in increasing the rationality of voting decisions. Such a definition implies that a voter makes a more rational choice the more clearly he discerns what is at stake in a particular election and the more consistent are the values he sees implicated in it. It implies also that a voting decision made on the basis of only a small part of available information about its consequences for goals valued by the voter is less rational than one taken when greater use is made of such information.

Rationality and Discussion

The two observations mentioned above suggest some of the features of a discussion that will contribute to rational voting. Before considering these, it may be worthwhile to note

[3] *Cf.* Herbert A. Simon, *Administrative Behavior* (1955), pp. 75-76.

how classical theories of free speech have treated the relation
between discussion and the rationality of community decisions. The notion that discussion can increase rationality of
choice is, of course, an integral part of such theories; and
basically there is nothing exceptional in this view—it is constantly acted on by all those who seek advice when they face
a hard decision. John Stuart Mill and other exponents of
the classical theory were arguing, simply, that men can take
counsel from public as well as private discussion and must
do so if their decisions are to be wise ones:

> The only way in which a human being can make some ap-
> proach to knowing the whole of a subject is by hearing what can
> be said about it by persons of every variety of opinion, and study-
> ing all modes in which it can be looked at by every character of
> mind. No wise man ever acquired his wisdom in any mode but
> this; nor is it in the nature of human intellect to become wise in
> any other manner.[4]

This is an argument for free speech strictly on the grounds
of its social utility. In Mill's view, public discussion was a
way in which citizens pooled information relevant to their
common affairs, exchanged opinions, and discovered truth
—particularly truth about the affairs of the community. Campaign discussion has been characterized in much the same
way, and for the same reasons, by those who attribute to it
an educational function. Like all public discussion, it is a
means by which the community can bring information to
bear on its political decisions. It provides, or can provide,
almost costless information to voters and can simplify their
task by directing attention only to those matters that will be
affected by their choices.[5]

The difficulty with most statements of this traditional conception of the relation of public discussion to rationality,

[4] John Stuart Mill, "On Liberty," in Edwin A. Burtt (ed.), *The English
Philosophers from Bacon to Mill* (1939), p. 964.
[5] *Cf.* Anthony Downs, *An Economic Theory of Democracy* (1957), pp. 216-17.

however, is that they imply that citizens are enlightened by any and all discussion. Since Mill's time students of politics have become less and less sure that the public discussion process would have quite so certain or so happy an ending as that which many of Mill's followers envisioned. Modern psychology has increasingly exposed the nonlogical and irrational components in human conduct, and its insights have been quickly assimilated and exploited by commercial and political propagandists. These developments do not in themselves negate Mill's reasoning—he was under no illusion that man was a wholly rational animal—but they have heightened awareness that not all talk increases the wisdom of the voter's decision, or of any decision. It must be talk of a certain kind.

A Model Campaign Discussion

What kind of discussion? This was the second question raised at the beginning of this chapter, and we can now attempt an answer. It should be noted at the outset that few generalizations can be made about the subject matter of a discussion that will contribute to rational action by voters. Almost any subject could be of concern to the electorate, although, following A. Lawrence Lowell, one can say that the voter needs mainly to know about men, measures, and parties.[6] The attitudes, temperaments, and competence of candidates; their policy commitments and intentions; their past actions in both public and private life; their party and other affiliations—all these matters may be relevant to the voter's decision.

None of these subjects is necessarily more important than the others, although the common tendency to condemn too

[6] See his *Public Opinion and Popular Government* (1921), pp. 71-85.

much emphasis on "personality" implies the contrary. Pendleton Herring has proposed a long list of legitimate interests that voters may have in the personality, personal characteristics, and personal ties of an office seeker:

> Is the candidate sincere? Does he seem honest and well meaning? Will he keep his promises? Who are his friends? Are they trustworthy people? What will the candidate do for me? Is he "my kind"? Does he stand for the same general social values and traditions that I cherish?[7]

Most of these questions would be important in any election, anywhere, but they are especially important in American elections, since the personality and personal qualifications of a candidate have much greater import for the future conduct of an officeholder in most constituencies in the United States than they do in a nation—or in the few American states— where there are more highly disciplined political parties. Furthermore, when elections are timed by the calendar, as they are in this country, they will often occur when policy issues of no great moment are at stake. In that event, the choice has to be mainly one between men and parties, not policies.

If little can be said about the subject matter of a discussion that will contribute to rationality in voting, something can be said about certain aspects of its content and of voter exposure to it. If a rational voting choice is one informed by an accurate knowledge of consequences, a discussion that will contribute to such choices must present, or enable the voter to arrive at, a reasonably accurate version of the subjects with which it deals. One that contained nothing but libels, false statements, and distortions could not conceivably aid rational decision making. The fewer such inaccuracies the discussion has, obviously, the more likely it is to facilitate rationality. It follows also that a discussion containing falsehoods and

---

[7] Pendleton Herring, *The Politics of Democracy* (1940), p. 289.

13

distortions will encourage rationality only to the extent that it also yields information that enables its audience to identify falsehoods and distortions. This last observation is important, because campaigns are a kind of adversary proceeding. Each party to the proceeding can be expected to distort: to put its case in the best possible light and its opponent's in the worst. Under such conditions the ability of the individual voter to get an accurate picture of the views and records of parties and candidates will depend to a large extent on whether or not he is exposed to the communications of both sides.

A second requirement that may be set for a discussion that will encourage rationality in voting would be this: It should expose the grounds on which candidates disagree and the differences between candidates—differences of personality, interest, affiliation, policy commitment, and all others that may affect performance in office. These differences need not be radical; indeed, they are unlikely to be in a two-party system. Nor does discussion have to dwell on differences and disagreements exclusively—something can be said for acknowledging, even at the height of the most vigorous campaign, that more unites the rival groups than separates them. Nevertheless, discussion should center on differences and disagreements, since only these provide a basis for choice. The more they are left undefined or are ambiguously defined, the less rational will the choice be.

The point can be made clearer by example. Suppose someone says, "The voters ought to re-elect Representative Jones, because he is a good family man, he belongs to five lodges, and he has seniority on the District of Columbia Committee." A controversy has begun as soon as another man has said, "I disagree." Nothing more is needed for a dispute—perhaps a long and heated one—but it will not be a dispute that can enlighten any decision, if it remains unclear on what grounds

14

the objector bases his disagreement. He may think that the congressman possesses none of these qualities or some but not others. He may think that the congressman possesses the qualities, but that they are unimportant. He may believe that the congressman possesses the qualities and that they are important and admirable, but also that the congressman has others that are highly undesirable. Unless the argument develops further around an issue like one of these, listeners will have no way of knowing in what respects the positions of the disputants differ and thus no basis for judging the merits of those positions.

Again, campaign discussion will contribute to rational decisions to the extent that those who participate in it offer reasons for preferring the policies or qualifications of one candidate to those of his opponent and that they subject such reasons to criticism, assessing their relevance, logical consistency, and the evidence on which they are based. Once a voter can see a difference in the positions taken by candidates, or in their personal characteristics, he must still decide which position, or which set of characteristics, is to be preferred. Campaign discussion should not only point up differences, but should help to clarify what difference the differences will make, since in the end the voter's decision must involve a judgment of value. For the electorate as a whole, this judgment will be better or worse depending on how thoroughly its members—or the decisive portion of them—have canvassed the reasons for and against voting for particular candidates. Once they have done so as well as they are able, nothing remains for them but to decide.

Finally, the model campaign discussion will be one in which the sources of the information that comes to the voter are clear. In campaigns the voter can and does receive valuable data from any number of places—the press, interest groups, nonpartisan organizations, party committees, candidates, or simply persons whose judgment he respects. These persons and agencies give information from quite different motives, however, and their statements are of varying significance and reliability. For these reasons, the voter will normally need to know who is speaking, and who is speaking for whom, before he can assign a value and meaning to any given piece of information.

All this is to suggest that campaign discussion contributes to the making of rational decisions by voters to the extent that it passes certain qualitative tests. Are voters exposed to the arguments of both sides? Does the discussion facilitate the identification of distortions and of false statements of fact? Are the candidates' statements of their views and intentions clear? Do candidates define their points of disagreement? Do campaigners offer evidence for their assertions and give reasons for favoring (or for having favored) particular policies? Are the sources of information clearly identified? If the answers to all these questions are "no," it is difficult to see how such a discussion could be expected to favor rational electoral action. If they are "yes," the probability that it will should be considerably increased.

Discussion and the Campaign Situation

It is common knowledge that campaign discussions meet at least some of the tests just proposed imperfectly. Can they be expected to meet them any better than they do? As has already been noted, many would argue that they cannot. The general form this argument takes has already been suggested and criticized, but it needs to be examined in more detail, for if it is correct, the model campaign discussion outlined above represents an unattainable ideal that is irrelevant to the evaluation of campaign discussion as it occurs.

The argument can be stated somewhat as follows: Given the nature of the campaign situation and the character and quality of the electorate, the shortcomings of campaign discussion are inevitable. Campaigns are struggles for power and the benefits of power. Campaigners are not seekers after truth in any sense that makes it at all likely that argument will alter their allegiances. The value of an argument to them will be its value in attracting attention, arousing the enthusiasm of partisans, and in winning support, and these may or may not coincide with its value as truth. If by exploiting the irrationality of the electorate, candidates will win votes, then they are under a compulsion to do so whenever votes to be won in this way seem likely to provide the margin of victory. The logical consistency of campaign statements depends, therefore, on the electorate's ability to appreciate logical consistency, the accuracy of such statements on the electorate's ability to recognize error, and their relevance on its ability to distinguish the trivial from the important. "The campaign methods that will be used," observes Pendleton Herring, "are those that prove their effectiveness. Political campaigning is concerned no more than commercial advertising with the plain unvarnished truth."[8] When there is emotionalism, sentimentality, distortion, and a poverty of ideas in campaign discussion, they are the natural outgrowth of the instrumental character of campaign communication and of the weaknesses of the electorate.

When examined, the argument is a good deal less convincing than it seems at first glance. It is, of course, true that the character of the electorate and the competitive nature of campaign communication are important influences on

[8] Herring, *op. cit.*, p. 269.

17

campaign discussion; but if Mill and other democratic theorists concluded that discussion would contribute to the wisdom of political decisions, it was not because they had ignored human irrationality, the force of arguments aimed at the irrational side of human nature, or the interest of politicians in making such arguments. Mill referred continually to those engaged in discussion as "advocates." He put down as the most common case of conflict of opinion that between partial versions of the truth. He acknowledged at one point that "the tendency of all opinions to become sectarian is not cured by the freest discussion, but is often heightened and exacerbated thereby; the truth which ought to have been, but was not, seen, being rejected all the more violently because proclaimed by persons regarded as opponents."[9] He also admitted the persuasive value of misrepresentation, the suppression of fact, invective, sarcasm, and attack on personality, and granted that "Men are not more zealous for truth than they often are for error."[10]

After making such concessions, one might regard Mill's confidence in the value of public discussion as something of a mystery, were it not for two further aspects of his argument. The first of these he stated explicitly: Public discussion was of value primarily to its audience, not to the discussants themselves. Collision of opinion works its salutary effect "not on the impassioned partisan" but "on the calmer and more disinterested bystander."[11] And it is realistic to assume that the electorate as a whole contains many more of the latter than the former. The second reason for Mill's optimism can be inferred from the language he chose to characterize discussion. He seems to have conceived of public controversies on political and social issues as being in the nature of debates, and to have equated the virtues of discussion developing out

[9] Mill, *op. cit.*, p. 989.
[10] *Ibid.*, p. 971.
[11] *Ibid.*, p. 989.

18

of such controversies with the virtues of discussion as it occurs in debate-like situations.[12] This is a most important, though almost undeveloped part of his argument, since the debating situation has important consequences for the character of the discussion that occurs there. In part this is true because some debating situations involve "rules of evidence and of parliamentary procedure . . . codes of fair dealing and fair comment."[13] More important, however, the conditions under which debates take place favor certain strategies of persuasion and render the use of others unwise.

Debate occurs when two parties advocating alternative courses of action bring their dispute before a common audience and ask that audience to favor one of the two proposals. Each of the disputants has an opportunity to state the reasoning that supports adoption of the alternative he recommends, and initially each will try to show that his proposals are in accordance with the principles, goals, and interests most cherished by the audience. Because the audience has heard his opponent's presentation as well as his own, however, it is to the debater's advantage to proceed to show the peculiar advantages of the action he recommends, for if he does not, his opponent will be able to claim "all this and more, too." The debater is under a compulsion to challenge those parts of his opponent's arguments that express aims or assumptions different from his own and must answer similar challenges from his opponent. If he does not, he risks a conclusion by the audience that his opponent's arguments cannot be

[12] For example, Mill chose four kinds of discussion techniques to illustrate the value of discussion, and they were all debate-like forms of discourse: The Socratic dialectic, Cicero's forensic practices, the school disputations of the Middle Ages, and the devil's advocate procedure employed by the Catholic Church at the canonization of saints. His consistent use of words and phrases like "adversary," "advocate," "refutation," "the reasons on the opposite side," "the arguments of opponents," "compulsion to hear both sides," and "judicial faculty," are further bits of evidence to support the inference that he saw public discussion as proceeding along the same lines as debate.

[13] As Walter Lippmann has suggested in *Essays in the Public Philosophy* (1956), p. 99.

challenged or that his own cannot be defended. If the debater replies to a challenge with too many obvious hedges, the audience may infer that his case is too weak to be frankly discussed. Discussion in debates progresses, therefore, from the debater's statement of a general position to his arguments for the particular aspects of that position that distinguish it from his opponent's.

The debating situation also sets up certain checks on the accuracy of the information that is brought to it. It is not advisable for a debater to misquote his opponent or to give an obviously distorted version of what his opponent has said. Members of the audience have heard his opponent's words for themselves, and the opponent can be counted on to call attention to the distortion. Neither is it advisable for the debater to base his attack on a false or distorted account of events—certainly not a distorted account that can be demonstrated as such—for he will risk exposure before all his listeners as a man who plays fast and loose with the facts. His opponent will have a strong incentive to point out distortion or falsehood, since it will be greatly to his advantage to show that an attempt has been made to mislead the audience.

Two of the morals to be drawn from this analysis should lead one to conclude that attributing the low quality of campaign discussion entirely to the weaknesses of the electorate and to the instrumental nature of campaign communication is to explain too much with too little. The first is that the qualitative differences that distinguish discussion in debates from other special pleading do not derive from qualitative differences in the audiences for debates; they are attributable instead to certain features of the debating situation. There is, therefore, no one-to-one relationship between the quality of a discussion and the character and quality of those to whom it is directed. The second moral is that there is no irreconcilable conflict between the interest of special pleaders in persuasive effectiveness and the interest of their audience in information that will help it assess their cases rationally. It would be foolish, of course, to pretend that debates leave no room for spurious arguments or for rhetoric to overcome reason. Nevertheless, in contrast to many other situations in which special pleading occurs, their general effect is to promote rational discourse, and they do so by making it in the debaters' interest to contribute to that kind of discussion. That the participants in public discussion may put effectiveness before truth is not something that in and of itself means that they cannot be made to serve truth.

But another conclusion also follows from what has been said. If Mill was equating public discussion with discussion as it occurs in debate, his conclusions must be read with one substantial qualification in mind. Only certain kinds of public discussion will take a debating form, because debate and the kind of discussion it encourages are based on a special relationship of the debaters to each other and to their audience. In a debating situation, the parties to a dispute enjoy equal access to an identical audience and equal abilities to communicate their arguments to that audience. These two characteristics of the debating situation account for much of what happens there. If they are not naturally present in the campaign situation, campaign discussion cannot be expected to assume a debate-like form.

Generally, students of politics have recognized that some kind of equality in the abilities of opposing candidates and parties to communicate is an essential presupposition of democratic government. Pendleton Herring, for example, bases a tolerant view of most modern propaganda practices on the assumption that cultivation of opinion need not be feared "so long as the gardeners continue to compete."[14] Two more

[14] Herring, *op. cit.,* p. 261.

recent writers observe that the American campaigners will never duplicate the mood of Nuremberg or Red Square so long as there are "two sets of loudspeakers, each of which is prepared to call the other a liar if it strays too far from the truth."[15] The only comment that need be added, perhaps, is that many of those who have adopted this view have been too ready to conclude that American political communication is in fact genuinely competitive.

That the quality of discussion is also determined in part by the relation of the discussants to each other and to their audiences has been less widely noted. Walter Lippmann has been one of the few to regard it as significant in this way and, before him, Ostrogorski. In 1902, the latter wrote regretfully of the passing of face-to-face debates from American political life. These, he observed, had allowed citizens "to grasp then and there the arguments pro and con presented by public men," while the political rallies that had supplanted them had as an object "not so much to instruct and convert as to edify the audience, to strengthen them in the party creed."[16] In another place he remarked that newspaper reports of speeches delivered in rallies, even when these gave adequate coverage to opposing sides, were no substitute for gatherings

> . . . at which people argue face to face. After all the fact is that in the meetings it is a case of preaching to converts, and that their sole object is to besprinkle the audience with the magnetic party fluid, to kindle the ardour which is smouldering within them, or, to use the favorite term by which leaders of the caucuses express their favorite idea, to "raise enthusiasm," or at least to convey the illusion of it to the public.[17]

[15] Austin Ranney and Willmoore Kendall, *Democracy and the American Party System* (1956), p. 359.
[16] M. Ostrogorski, *Democracy and the Organization of Political Parties* (1902), Vol. II, pp. 317-19.
[17] *Ibid.*, Vol. I, p. 391.

Problems of Campaign Discussion

The course of the argument to this point may be summarized as follows: The social objective of campaign discussion is to encourage rational voting. Discussion will further this objective to the extent that it clarifies differences between candidates; presents reasons for adopting alternative courses of action; comes from clearly identified sources: exposes voters to the arguments of both sides; and gives the voter an accurate view of the subjects with which it deals. If campaign discussion cannot be made to meet these specifications more fully than it now does, it is not for the reasons most frequently used to justify pessimism about the possibility of improving its quality. The present shortcomings of campaign discussion cannot be attributed solely to the nature of the campaign situation or to the shortcomings of the electorate.

This conception of the relation between campaign discussion and rationality in voting diverges in some respects from both of the principal views of this relation current in American political thought. One of these, which finds expression in the work of many who have made empirical studies of campaigning, has assumed almost as given the inappropriateness of campaign discussion to the rational consideration of issues. The other has extolled free public discussion in terms that imply the enlightenment of the public as its natural and inevitable consequence. This latter tendency owes much to the fact that the freedom of speech, press, and assembly are enshrined in the American Constitution.

If the reasoning above is correct, however, it should be apparent that one can easily be led astray by either of these attitudes. The value of discussion in campaigns is conditional

—what is said there can mislead or enlighten voters. Which of these things it does will depend partly on the form the discussion takes, and this will vary in different kinds of discussion situations. Raising the level of campaign discussion is not an inherently unrealizable goal. Its realization does entail difficult technical and political problems at every step, as the foregoing analysis has implied.

One of these problems, certainly, is how to ensure the access and exposure of the electorate to the arguments on all sides of significant questions and to the rival claims of those who attempt to lead it. Protecting the rights of opposing forces to speak and publish freely is only a part of the solution. If the public is to hear both sides, both sides must have comparable abilities to make themselves heard. This has never been a certain result of free speech or even of the party system, which has institutionalized the presentation to the electorate of alternative sets of candidates and policy proposals. It is particularly uncertain in a society where costs of access to communication media become greater and greater, and where political leaders must compete for the electorate's attention, not only with each other, but with thousands of distracting stimuli.

Achieving a political discourse that is valuable as well as competitive is an even more difficult practical problem. One need not seek far to find instances in campaign discussion of distortion, falsehood, irrelevancy, ambiguity, and evasion that make extremely doubtful its contributions to rational electoral action. If such abuses do not inevitably need to infect campaigning to the extent they do presently, neither will they disappear unless ways can be found to channel campaign discussion into forms that are appropriate to an educational objective.

False and libelous attacks on candidates are another feature of American political life that subverts the value of campaign discussion. Such attacks are only one form of falsehood and distortion; but they are a particularly damaging one, since the personal merits of candidates must always be an important consideration to American voters. They are an old problem[18] complicated today by the size of modern electorates and the growing use of mass communication techniques in political campaigns.

The voter's difficulty in assessing the reliability of his sources of information makes the potential benefits of free discussion problematic in still another way. Walter Lippmann has called detection of the disguised partisan one of the most perplexing problems of popular government and has observed that: "The separation of the public from the self-interested group will not be assisted by the self-interested group."[19] This fact is nowhere more apparent than in political campaigns, in which anonymous literature, "front" organizations, and planted propaganda have all been used to mask the fact or character of interested attempts to persuade.

These problems may now be examined in detail.

[18] In 1890, Bryce asked English readers to "Imagine all the accusations brought against all the candidates for the 670 seats in the English parliament concentrated on one man, and read by sixty millions of people daily for three months, and you will still fail to realize what is the tempest of invective and calumny which hurtles round the head of a presidential candidate." James Bryce, *The American Commonwealth* (1890), Vol. II, p. 209.

[19] Walter Lippmann, *The Phantom Public* (1925), p. 113.

3

Access to Campaign Audiences

THE PRECEDING CHAPTER suggested that campaigners on both sides should enjoy comparable access to the voter's attention if campaign discussion is to encourage rationality in voting. This is an obvious requirement for any kind of government by consent, but not one that seems to be met well in practice. In the few campaigns for which we have reliable information on the exposure of voters to campaign communication, campaign audiences tended to be segmented; that is, audiences for rival candidates tended to be separate audiences. The campaign audiences also tended to have a highly variable membership—voters gave discontinuous attention to campaign discussion.

Audience exposure of this kind, of course, would not maximize the rationality of electoral decisions. When the campaign audience is segmented, rival candidates may be real competitors for victory at the polls, but they are not competitors for the favor of individual voters. Voting blocs confront each other on election day; alternative views do not confront each other in the voter's mind. When, further, the audience has a variable membership, most voters cannot be depended on to relate the different parts of any individual candidate's case, nor the challenges of one candidate to the replies of another. They are therefore not in a position to sum up the advantages that would attend voting for each candidate and strike a balance between them.

Thus, those who would design a program to increase rationality in voting must face the fact of segmentation and variable membership in the campaign audience, must seek to determine its causes, and must try to find measures to combat it. Before discussing causes and remedies, however, it will be worthwhile to review the evidence for the existence of the problem. This evidence is not so extensive as might be desired, but all of it points in the same direction.

Audience Exposure to Campaign Communication

Direct evidence that many voters were much more heavily exposed to the communications of one side—usually the side they favored—has been reported in three studies of campaign communication, and the same tendency was found in a fourth study, though to a much lesser degree.[1] In their study of voting in Erie County, Ohio, for instance, Lazarsfeld and his co-workers found that 54 per cent of those classed as predisposed to vote Republican were exposed mainly to Republican propaganda, 35 per cent were exposed mainly to Democratic propaganda, and only 11 per cent had a balanced exposure. The comparable figures for voters predisposed to vote Democratic were 61 per cent with a mainly Democratic exposure, 22 per cent with a mainly Republican exposure, and 17 per cent with balanced exposure.

Two of the principal studies of voting behavior have also reported direct evidence that the campaign audience has a

[1] See Paul F. Lazarsfeld, Bernard Berelson, and Hazel Gaudet, *The People's Choice* (1948), pp. 80-84; Ruth Ziff, "The Effect of the Last Three Weeks of a Presidential Campaign on the Electorate" (Columbia University, M.A. thesis, 1948); and Department of Marketing, Miami University, *The Influence of Television on the Election of 1952* (1954), p. 39. It was Bernard Berelson, Paul F. Lazarsfeld, and William N. McPhee who found the tendency less pronounced. See *Voting* (1954), p. 245.

highly variable membership. Berelson, Lazarsfeld, and Mc-Phee, summarizing their findings on this point, observe that campaign exposure "seems to be of two kinds: (1) the heavy exposure of the few really 'attending' to the campaign; and (2) the moderate exposure of the many 'also present.' "[2] Lazarsfeld and his co-workers in Erie County had reported previously that "the people who were exposed to a lot of campaign propaganda through one medium of communication were also exposed to a lot in other media; and those who were exposed to a little in one were exposed to a little in others."[3]

A similar picture of the campaign audience as both segmented and of changing membership can be drawn from radio and television audience survey data. Were the campaign audience not of this character, it is reasonable to infer that the size of the audiences for the major policy speeches of any one candidate would not vary greatly, and that there would be no great discrepancy in the size of the audiences for the speeches of rival candidates. This, however, is not the case. During the 1952 presidential campaign the number of television homes reached by Eisenhower speeches varied from 236,000 to 7,300,000. The average number of sets tuned to an Eisenhower speech was a little over 4,120,000. The number of television homes reached by Stevenson speeches also varied widely yielding an average of 3,620,000. For radio, the figures were comparable.[4]

The data just noted all relate to audience exposure to propaganda emanating from the mass media, but information on the character of face-to-face communication in campaigns gives no more of a basis for assuming that candidates enjoy

[2] Berelson, Lazarsfeld, and McPhee, *Voting*, p. 245.
[3] Lazarsfeld, Berelson, and Gaudet, *The People's Choice*, p. 122.
[4] See Charles A. H. Thomson, *Television and Presidential Politics* (1956), pp. 57-58 and Stanley Kelley, Jr., *Professional Public Relations and Political Power* (1956), p. 197.

either equal or adequate access to voters' attention. Party workers make personal contact with a relatively small part of the electorate,[5] and most of these contacts are with voters who share the party workers' allegiances and sympathies.[6] Similarly, informal political discussion does less than might be supposed to expose voters to opposing viewpoints:

> At the height of the campaign . . . political discussion on the grass roots level apparently consists more of the exchange of mutually agreeable remarks than of controversial ones. The process of clarifying and modifying views with opponents that is assumed to constitute the give-and-take of informal political debate throughout the community is not predominant during the presidential campaign.[7]

An Explanation

Berelson, Larzarsfeld, and McPhee have constructed the most convincing explanation of the campaign audience's variable membership. Among voters with a low degree of interest in political affairs, variations in the numbers of those exposed to campaign propaganda can be expected to vary with the volume of propaganda directed to them.[8] This means that the opportunities of campaign organizations to communicate will be an important factor in determining the extent to which voters enter the campaign audience. When the interest factor is controlled, exposure seems to vary with the voter's social

---

[5] The Survey Research Center reported that the votes of only 12 per cent of its panel were solicited by party workers in the course of the 1952 presidential campaign. Angus Campbell, Gerald Gurin, and Warren E. Miller, *The Voter Decides* (1954), p. 33.

[6] Berelson, Lazarsfeld, and McPhee found that ". . . party contact was selectively directed not toward the joining of political issues in discussion or debate on the level of the individual voter. Rather it was directed toward the agreeable (noncontroversial) exploitation of existing strength." *Voting*, p. 174.

[7] *Ibid.*, p. 106.

[8] *Ibid.*, p. 245.

awareness, education, subjective feelings about his stake in the community, social role (women pay less attention to campaign discussion than men), and personal adjustment.[9]

An equally convincing explanation of the tendency of the campaign audience to segment is harder to formulate. Lazarsfeld, Berelson, and Gaudet have pointed to the voter himself as the primary source of the difficulty. In their view, the voter's unequal exposure to competing campaign appeals derives from his tendency to select out for attention those appeals that conform most nearly to his own ideas. He seeks to reinforce his existing convictions, not to learn. "[The voter] has a readiness to attend to some things more than others. His internal situation as well as his external situation is weighted one way or the other. Voters somehow contrive to select out of the passing stream of stimuli those by which they are now inclined to be persuaded."[10]

Undoubtedly, this tendency of voters to hear what they want to hear exists and is one factor that encourages the segmentation of the campaign audience. By itself, however, it is not enough to explain the electorate's unequal exposure to partisan propaganda (nor do the authors' of *The People's Choice* regard it as such). In the first place, Lazarsfeld and his co-workers found that a considerable proportion of the persons predisposed to vote Republican had been exposed mainly to Democratic campaign messages and vice versa. In these cases the predispositions of voters were obviously not the cause of unequal exposure. Secondly, the explanation of these authors fails to take account of the fact that what is communicated will affect the voter's disposition to attend or not to attend to communications.

This last point suggests a second explanation that can be given for audience segmentation. The content of campaign

[9] *Ibid.*, p. 241.
[10] Lazarsfeld, Berelson, and Gaudet, *The People's Choice*, pp. 81-82.

discussion encourages voters to listen mainly to the side they favor. In point of fact, much campaign propaganda is not meant to attract the interest of opposition supporters. The American political rally, Harold Lasswell has observed, "is a situation in which speeches are secular sermons. The speakers do not expect to disagree with one another, and they do not expect to be disagreed with by the audience. . . . They celebrate unity."[11] The aim of such communication is to mobilize sentiment, to appeal to the party member's feeling of belonging, not to convert. It is not surprising, therefore, that it should repel, as well as attract, audiences. The logical consequence of the stategy of mobilization is to build separate audiences for rival candidates.

This strategy, moreover, has its roots in the economics of propaganda. Other things being equal, it is less costly in time, effort, and money to conform to existing opinion than it is to change it, cheaper to mobilize existing sentiment than it is to build new sentiment. The fewer resources that campaign organizations can devote to persuasion and the more costly communications become, therefore, the more any attempts to convert opposition partisans become a luxury. This is precisely the logic that campaign organizations adopt in their canvassing activities. Normally, the canvasser's objective is to contact voters of his own party first, then independents, and then—and only then—opposition voters.

The strategy of mobilization, however, would not account for the fact that some voters predispose, to vote for one party are exposed mainly to the propaganda of the other. At least for this particular kind of audience segmentation, a third explanation is the most plausible one: The passivity of voters enables campaign organizations to capture the more or less exclusive attention of a certain number of them, when either one or both parties lack the resources to reach the total elec-

[11] Harold D. Lasswell, *Democracy Through Public Opinion* (1941), pp. 85-86.

torate with their campaign messages. If rival campaign organizations enjoy comparable opportunities to communicate, they will make comparable numbers of voters their captives; if they are unequal in their opportunities to communicate, their captives will also be unequal in numbers.

Given available evidence, one cannot demonstrate any positive correlation between the relative opportunities of candidates and parties to communicate and their relative success in capturing voters. Only fragmentary information exists on the access of candidates and parties to the channels of communication—fragmentary in that it concerns only a few media and a few campaigns.[12] It is possible that unequal and inadequate

[12] It is known, of course, that the campaign expenditures reported by the two major parties have shown substantial advantages for Republican presidential candidates. The Republicans, at least since 1920, have outspent the Democrats in ratios varying from 3.68 to 1 in 1924 to 1.17 to 1 in 1928. (See Louise Overacker, *Money in Elections*, 1932, p. 75; Miss Overacker's articles in the *American Political Science Review*, Vol. 35, August 1941, p. 705 and Vol. 39, October 1945, p. 906; and the testimony of Alexander Heard in *1956 Presidential and Senatorial Campaign Contributions and Practices*, Hearings before the Senate Committee on Rules and Administration, 84 Cong. 2 sess., Pt. 2, pp. 239-49.) If expenditures can be taken as rough indicators of opportunity to communicate, then the parties have been unequal in this respect in the period 1920-1952.

Through the work of Alexander Heard we have a more refined notion of communication expenditures in the 1952 presidential campaign. Heard found eighteen political committees supporting Eisenhower to have made total expenditures for publicity and propaganda of about $3,102,000. The comparable figure for groups supporting Adlai Stevenson was $2,858,000. (Alexander Heard, *op. cit.*, pp. 246-49.) Heard's figures are the most reliable measure available of the extent to which the two parties were able to put paid messages into communication channels in any recent campaign. They include expenditures for recording, printing, campaign buttons, advertising "gimmicks," direct mail, newspaper advertising, photography, movie production and projection, and billboard and poster advertising—all forms of communication for which other indications of the nature and extent of production and distribution are lacking.

In 1956 the Senate Subcommittee on Privileges and Elections reported somewhat greater expenditures for publicity by national committees supporting the Democrats ($3,197,330) and by Labor ($214,133) than by national committees supporting the Republicans ($2,430,985). See Senate Committee on Rules and Administration, *1956 General Election Campaigns*, Report, 85 Cong. 1 sess. (1957), pp. 39-40.

opportunities to communicate will lead to unequal exposure, however; and clearly, too, campaign organizations do attempt to execute a strategy of capture. Appeals to passive or "stay-at-home" voters play an important part in campaigning and are disseminated in spot announcement campaigns, in film riders on popular commercial television shows, and in massive amounts of campaign literature.[13]

If what has been said so far has been convincing, it should be evident that differential opportunities to communicate, the content of communications, and the predispositions of voters all need to be considered in explaining the unequal exposure of the electorate to competing propaganda. If this is so, and if the variable membership of the campaign audience is partially dependent on the volume of propaganda campaign organizations generate, some aspects of a strategy to change the character of audience exposure in a way that will encourage rationality in voting become apparent. The points of attack must be on the content of campaign communication and on those factors that determine the opportunities of candidates and parties to communicate. Discussion of measures that might be taken to change the content of campaign discussion is reserved for a later chapter, but in the remainder of this one we shall examine what has been done to give campaign organizations a comparable chance to reach voters and some further measures that might be taken to that end.

[13] A public relations blueprint prepared for the 1952 Republican presidential campaign set winning votes among so-called "stay-at-home" voters as one of its high priority goals. Why? "The pertinent fact," argued the authors of the blueprint, "is that Stay-at-Homes outnumber the Independents by approximately forty-five million to an estimated three or four million." (Quoted in the author's *Professional Public Relations and Political Power* 1956, p. 155.) Immediately after his 1956 nomination, Adlai Stevenson, speaking to the members of the Democratic National Committee, similarly stressed the need to reach the stay-at-home vote, characterizing it as possibly decisive. *New York Times*, Aug. 19, 1956.

Election Law and the Opportunity to Communicate

American legislators have shown little interest in helping campaigners to make their views known to voters as an end in itself, but they have been concerned about the possible consequences of unequal opportunities to disseminate partisan propaganda, even in the absence of precise information on the magnitude of the problem. Congress has taken two steps to equalize such opportunities, one direct, the other indirect. Several states have also tried to put remedies into their election codes.

Partisan favoritism by broadcasters, an obvious potential source of unequal opportunities to communicate, is forbidden by Section 315 of the Federal Communications Act. Section 315 provides that: "If any licensee shall permit any person who is a legally qualified candidate for any public office to use a broadcasting station, he shall afford equal opportunities to all other such candidates for that office in the use of such broadcasting station." Section 315 does not mean, of course, that the holder of a broadcasting license must give time gratis to candidates. Rather he must deal with rival candidates on equal terms. If he gives one candidate free time, he must also make free time available to the candidate's opponents. If he sells a candidate time, he is required to stand ready to sell comparable time to the opposition candidate or candidates at the same price. Candidates are guaranteed equal time on the air if they want it and if they can pay for it.[14]

[14] Congress has recently made it clear that coverage of the activities of candidates in bona fide newscasts, news documentaries, or news interview programs does not give their rivals claim to equal time (Public Law 274, 73 Stat. 557). It did so by amending Section 315 to this effect after the Federal Communications Commission held on February 19, 1959, that some film clips of Mayor Richard J. Daley used in a news broadcast by a Chicago television station during the Chicago mayoralty primary entitled his primary opponent, Lar Daly, to equal time.

34

Unequal financial resources are another obvious potential source of unequal opportunities for rival campaign organizations to communicate. Talk is not cheap when it is done on any extensive scale, as it must be in modern campaigns. Contemporary campaign communication in contests for federal and many state and municipal offices is almost necessarily mass communication—that is, it is directed toward, and intended to influence, large groups of people. The mass media make it possible to reach these large audiences, but they are expensive, and their costs have been steadily rising. Whether these developments have been balanced by a rise in the income of political organizations is not determinable in an exact way, but it is the judgment of Alexander Heard that: "Income and gift taxes as well as limitations on lump sum contributions now make the filling of campaign chests far more complicated than in earlier days."[15]

The size of a candidate's campaign chest is, of course, one measure of his financial resources, but not the only important one. The amount of money available to him will be one of the main factors in determining the volume of his propaganda, his freedom to choose the form that propaganda will take, and the kind of professional advice he can obtain in planning and executing his propaganda strategy. The high costs of access to mass communication facilities, however, mean that relatively small differences in the total amount of money available to candidates can result in great differences in their opportunities to reach voters. For something over $9,000 one may speak to a nationwide television audience for five minutes; for about $7,500 one may be able to reach a comparable audience for only a few seconds or a considerably smaller audience for the same length of time. High costs of access also make the flow of funds extremely important to the campaigner. Even if at the end of a campaign two candidates

[15] Alexander Heard, *Money and Politics* (1956), p. 21.

35

have spent similar amounts, one may have had to use less effective propaganda methods or to delay speeches beyond the opportune moment, because he did not have the right amount of money at the right time.[16]

Unequal financial resources as a source of unequal opportunities to communicate are dealt with—in theory at least—by those provisions in both federal and state election laws placing limitations on the aggregate expenditures of candidates and political committees. The Federal Corrupt Practices Act sets limits on the amount of money that may be spent by candidates for the Senate and for the House of Representatives, and Section 20 of the Hatch Political Activities Act seeks to limit expenditures in campaigns for the presidency by prohibiting any national political committee to spend or collect funds in excess of $3,000,000. The provisions of state law vary. In some states, the law itself may fix a dollar maximum. In others, the allowable expenditure may be computed as a fixed percentage of the salary of the office sought. In still others, the maximum may be arrived at by multiplying numbers of voters—usually the number of votes cast in the preceding election—by a fixed sum.

In the application of laws of this kind, the legitimacy of any given expenditure is not in question. Their purpose is to achieve some kind of balance in the abilities of contending parties and candidates to compaign, "to give worth and ability an even show in the race for public office as against trickery, cunning, and money."[17] Since communication is the most expensive single aspect of campaigning, expenditure ceilings may also be regarded as setting limits on the opportunities of any one candidate or political committee to communicate,

[16] This is particularly true in broadcasting, where stations and networks usually require full payment in advance.

[17] From Justice James F. Ailshie's concurring opinion interpreting the Idaho Statute, *Adams* v. *Lansdom*, 18 Idaho 483 (1910), pp. 511-12.

and have been advocated as a way of equalizing such opportunities.[18]

State sponsored, state subsidized voters' pamphlets have been a third kind of remedy for inequalities in the opportunity to communicate attempted by legislators. Oregon law, for instance, directs the Secretary of State to prepare a pamphlet that will present arguments supporting and opposing candidacies and ballot measures. The arguments are submitted by party committees, by independent candidates, persons, or organizations filing initiative petitions, and by any persons opposing candidacies or ballot measures. Within a specified time before each primary and general election, the pamphlet is mailed to all the state's registered voters. The persons and organizations submitting material pay about one third of the production and distribution costs, and the state pays the rest. Two other states have followed in part the Oregon example: California distributes a ballot measure pamphlet and North Dakota uses a candidate pamphlet for primary elections.

All these measures—Section 315, federal and state legislation limiting aggregate expenditures, and voters' pamphlets

[18] Such a view was taken, for instance, by Professor Karl Lowenstein in a statement to the Senate Subcommittee on Privileges and Elections: "Elections, even if fair and honest from the technical viewpoint of organizing and conducting the ballot, may result in a distorted reflection of the electoral will unless equal chances are afforded the parties and candidates in electoral propaganda. In a mass society the individual voter is able to inform himself about issues and personalities exclusively through the media of communications. If these are used by an individual party or candidate to a larger extent than by others, the individual voter is exposed to a disproportionate intellectual pressure that cannot but affect adversely his judgment. For these reasons equality of electioneering chances is the indispensable basis of honest democratic elections." (See *Federal Elections Act of 1955*, Hearings before the Senate Committee on Rules and Administration, 84 Cong. 1 sess., p. 295.) Professor Lowenstein's rationale for expenditure ceilings is of course not the only one that has been offered for laws setting limits on total campaign expenditures. Others have argued that ceilings discourage corrupt practices like treating and bribery, that they lessen the dependence of candidates on large contributors, and that they eliminate waste in campaign expenditures.

—are directed toward limited aspects of the task of ensuring candidates a comparable access to channels of communication and the campaign audience. The first two have serious defects even as partial remedies. Only the third appears to be an efficient means to that end.

There have been no serious complaints that Section 315 has been ineffective in preventing discriminatory treatment of candidates by broadcast license holders. Criticisms of the law arise chiefly from the fact that it has discouraged station managements from granting free time to candidates. Why? Essentially because Section 315 assumes all candidates are equal. This means that any grant of free time to major party candidates during an election campaign makes all legally qualified candidates of minor parties eligible to receive comparable time without cost. It means that any free time given leading candidates for nomination in a primary campaign opens station managements to demands for equal time by all other candidates for the same nomination, no matter how frivolous their candidacy. The reaction of broadcasters is a quite natural one:

> How many . . . have heard of Homer A. Tomlinson or Fred C. Proehl or Don DuMont or Edward Longstreet Bodin or Ellen Linea W. Jensen? Each of these was a duly nominated candidate for President in 1952. There were, in all, 18 political parties with presidential candidates in 1952. . . . No matter how obscure many of these parties may be, section 315 requires us to regard them on an equal footing with the Democratic and Republican parties. We cannot, therefore, consider giving a half hour free to the Republican and Democratic candidates without taking into account the 16 more half hours which under the law we would be required to give to the other 16 parties at their request . . . As a matter of simple common sense, in the interests of our own self preservation as well as the protection of our listeners . . . once the campaign actually begins, we cannot give time free to candidates; we must sell it at regular rates.[19]

[19] Testimony of Richard S. Salant, Vice President, Columbia Broadcasting System, in *Federal Elections Act of 1955*, Hearings before the Senate Committee on Rules and Administration, 84 Cong. 1 sess., pp. 175-76.

Thus, Section 315 really gives candidates a quite fictitious equality in access to the airwaves because it reduces the willingness of broadcasters to give free time and therefore makes the candidate's ability to pay the principal factor that determines the extent of his time on the air.[20] It probably also reduces the ability of all major party candidates to reach voters.

Granting that minor parties have a claim on the conscience of the majority, if not on its allegiance, Section 315 benefits them little, if at all, and operates to the practical detriment of the major parties. The difference between guaranteeing all parties and candidates an equal right to speak—that is, the opportunity to spread their doctrines without legal interference —and guaranteeing them equal access to the mass media of communication is in this instance very apparent. British election law shows a more pragmatic approach to this kind of problem than our own. Hyde Park is a symbol of the British tolerance and protection of the rights of minority party spokesmen to speak freely. In English election campaigns, however, it is the two major parties that are given equal access to radio and television facilities, while minor parties are allotted time in a way that reflects roughly their electoral significance.

Provisions limiting the expenditures of candidates and political committees have been found even less satisfactory than Section 315. Both practicing politicians and students of government have criticized these measures as inefficacious in practice and ill advised in principle. Philip L. Graham, publisher of the *Washington Post and Times Herald,* speaking before a

[20] In the period from September 1 to November 6, 1956, networks gave 32 hours, and local stations something over 185 hours, of free time for campaign broadcasts. Charles A. H. Thomson comments, ". . . if these figures are deflated by the number of stations (450) and the number of candidates (very large) they lose impressiveness, and comport more closely with the claims of the networks that they cannot give substantial free time for political broadcasting during campaigns, even for the key offices of President and Vice President." "Television, Politics, and Public Policy," *Public Policy,* Vol. 8 (1958), p. 374.

congressional committee, attacked existing federal expenditure ceilings as calculated to make politicians "practical hypocrites."[21] His view is not one peculiar to himself. Students of political finance have found these laws rarely honored in their spirit and often not in their letter.

In the present context, it is more important to state the theoretical than the practical criticism. Large sums of money can be spent for legitimate campaign purposes. The publicizing of issues and candidates to an electorate as large as that involved in many campaigns is necessarily expensive. If limitations on expenditures were in fact used to equalize the opportunities of candidates to communicate and to campaign, it would be necessary to fix the upper limit at so low a figure that any candidate with considerable support would be able to spend to that limit. To do this, however, would almost certainly impair the efficacy of campaigns as institutions of public discussion. Louise Overacker concluded from her study of campaign finance that "the real danger is not that some spend too much, but that others spend too little."[22] The point may be paraphrased here: The danger—at least from the public's point of view—is not that some politicians will talk too much, but that others will be able to say too little.

Rather than adopting this view of campaign expenditures, legislators have been prone to consider large-scale spending as an evil in itself, and therefore as something to be kept in check. In the field of communications, they would do much better to think in terms of minimums—the minimum requirements for assuring rival candidates opportunities to win access to the attention of the total electorate, at least at some stage in the selection process that leads to public office. Equality of expenditures at low levels may bring some equality in the opportunities of candidates to communicate, but it will

[21] Dec. 12, 1956.
[22] Louise Overacker, *Money in Elections* (1932), p. 96.

not reduce segmentation in the campaign audience or work to bring more voters into the campaign audience.

Something like this reasoning has been adopted by the legislatures of those states that sponsor voters' pamphlets. The original advocates of the Oregon candidate pamphlet asked its adoption as a means to "give poor men an equal chance with the men who are supported by wealth in aspiring for nomination and election to public office."[23] It must be regarded not only as having been partially successful in doing so, but also in enlarging the audience for campaign discussion and in combating its tendency to segment.

Whitaker and Baxter, who have managed dozens of California initiative and referendum campaigns, have this to say about that state's pamphlet:

> We consider the Voters' Pamphlet an exceedingly valuable campaign medium. It has been our experience that in California this is often the most widely read publication of the campaign. We have taken surveys in former years to test this theory and have found that tens of thousands of families, on the Saturday or Sunday before a Tuesday election, gather in the family living room to go over arguments for and against ballot issues.[24]

Another California public relations man, Thomas S. Page, offers a similar judgment:

> I consider the voters' handbook, as we call it, one of the most important, if not the most important, documents of a campaign.
>
> A campaign runs through time—and as it approaches its end, it runs away from the campaigner, and all he can do is watch it hit. This starts to happen about a week before election day—his job is nearly done. And one of the places the campaign hits is in the voters' book. My hunch is that more than 50 per cent of all the voters use the voters' book to study those issues and those candidates who are controversial, and as to which a real decision will be made.

[23] See Robert C. Brooks, *Political Parties and Electoral Problems* (1923), pp. 248-50.

[24] In a letter to the author.

This time of study, and this moment of decision, comes in the closing week. I know of no other document which plays area-wide such an important role in that dreadful word "the decision-making process."[25]

Other professional campaigners in California share these views,[26] and, in correspondence with the writer, seven of the nine members of the Oregon and North Dakota delegations to Congress praised the pamphlet as an important and effective campaign device.[27] The Oregon Legislative Interim Committee on Elections found this attitude adopted by voters and candidates generally in that state.[28]

Candidates and professional campaigners not only have similar opinions of the voters' pamphlet, but similar reasons for those opinions. The pamphlet makes a campaign organization's argument available to every voter. Its official character gives it a special claim to the voter's attention, as does the fact that it gives him an opportunity to see presentations of both sides in a single place.[29] It allows the campaign organization this kind of access to the voter at no cost, or at very moderate cost. For these same reasons the pamphlet recommends itself as a partial solution to the problems under discussion here.

[25] In a letter to the author.
[26] D. V. Nicholson and Herbert Baus, both of whom have long experience as professional campaign managers.
[27] The remaining two did not respond to the inquiry.
[28] Letter to the author from A. Freeman Holmer, Executive Secretary of the Legislative Interim Committee.
[29] Whitaker and Baxter observe: "The key reason for the effectiveness of this Pamphlet is that it affords the voter an opportunity to study both sides of the case, presented simultaneously in the same document, under official auspices." (Letter to the author.) Herbert Baus stresses that "This pamphlet is a most useful form of persuasion, because it is considered 'official' and I believe a large number of voters who pay little attention to anything else make an effort to study this document." Letter to the author.

Legal Action to Promote Discussion

Both politicians and students of politics have suggested a number of new measures designed to promote campaign discussion and to ensure its competitive character. The proposals most frequently advanced involve revision of the laws limiting aggregate expenditures, either repeal or revision of Section 315, and providing government subsidies for campaign activities. The shortcomings of the first class of proposals have already been noted. It is useful at this point to discuss the latter two, however, though more will have to be said about them when further considerations are introduced in later chapters.

There is widespread support for changes of some kind in Section 315 both among political party leaders and network officials. Spokesmen for CBS, NBC, and ABC have all gone on record against Section 315 in its present form, and various revisions of it have been sponsored by members of both parties in Congress. A few of those who want a change advocate outright repeal, others favor measures that would require the networks to give free time to candidates, and still others would alter the provisions of Section 315 that give equal claims on time to major and minor parties, to serious and trivial candidates.

Charles A. H. Thomson has given one of the most thoughtful analyses of these proposed changes.[30] He rejects repeal of Section 315 as a step that would delegate excessive political power and responsibility to broadcasters. He also rejects the idea that stations ought to be forced to give free time to candidates: "If the government were to force the networks to give

[30] Charles A. H. Thomson, *Television and Presidential Politics* (1956), pp. 125-34; and "Television, Politics and Public Policy," *Public Policy*, Vol. 8 (1958), pp. 368-406.

up enough time to accommodate everybody, this would amount to a taking of property (not access to the spectrum, but the right to sell time over broadcasting stations.)"[31] The most important single way to promote the political use of television on an equitable basis, in his view, is to restrict the application of the equal time provisions of the present law to candidates of major parties in general election campaigns and to leading candidates in nomination contests.

Such a proposal immediately raises a practical question— how can the terms "major party" and "leading candidate" be given an administratively sound definition? Thomson argues that adequate definitions of a major party have already been incorporated into state legislation regulating the eligibility of parties to use state machinery for primary elections. He grants that defining a "leading candidate" for a major party nomination is a more difficult problem, but offers the following as a tentative solution: "A leading candidate for a party nomination shall be deemed to be any candidate who is able, on demand, to adduce substantial evidence of his probable ability to secure at least 15 per cent of the vote on the first ballot of the party convention or primary in which the party nomination shall be made."[32] A candidate, in case of controversy, could offer evidence that he qualified for treatment as a leading candidate from at least four sources: "(1) reputable polling surveys, by Gallup and others; (2) extent of announced support by political leaders; (3) results in state primaries; and (4) expert opinion, based on these and other factors."[33]

Revisions along this line would remove the chief obstacle to the granting of free time to major party candidates and would augment their chances for increased access, on terms of equality, to radio and television facilities. Moreover, such re-

[31] Thomson, *Television and Presidential Politics*, p. 128.
[32] *Ibid.*, p. 132.
[33] *Ibid.*

visions would not necessarily mean that minor party candidates would have less opportunity to air their views than they now do. Separate provision could be made for them in a revised Section 315, perhaps one granting them time in amounts that would reflect their electoral strength. Even in the absence of such a provision, the more newsworthy of the minor parties would probably get more radio and television time than they now do if their access to it depended simply on the general obligation of station and network managers to provide public service programs.

Granting government subsidies for campaign activities, the second possible way to reduce inequalities in opportunities to communicate to be discussed here, is not a new idea. Theodore Roosevelt proposed a campaign subsidy in a message to Congress in 1907.[34] In recent years, Oregon's Senator Richard L. Neuberger introduced a bill that would provide federal contributions to the campaigns of the two major parties,[35] and the Commonwealth of Puerto Rico[36] has enacted a campaign

[34] He asked Congress to provide "an appropriation for the proper and legitimate expenses of each of the great national parties, an appropriation ample enough to meet the necessity for thorough organization and machinery, which requires a large expenditure of money. The stipulation should be made that no party receiving campaign funds from the Treasury should accept more than a fixed amount from any individual subscriber or donor. . . ." *Congressional Record*, Vol. 42, Pt. 1, 60 Cong. 1 sess., p. 78. Roosevelt seems to have felt that alternative systems of regulating campaign finance unduly penalized the honest politician.

[35] S. 3242, 84 Cong. 2 sess. The bill was co-sponsored by Senators Wayne Morse, James Murray, Paul Douglas, John Sparkman, Mike Mansfield, William Langer, and Hubert Humphrey.

[36] Act 110, approved June 30, 1957. The act declares it to be "a universally admitted principle that political parties are instruments necessary to democracy in that it is through them that the people lend their support to programs and express mandates with regard to their government" and that it is therefore "profoundly in the public interest" that these "democratic organizations be adequately provided the funds for the fulfillment of their most essential functions. . . ." Specific provisions of the act limit the expenditures that can be made in campaigns and the amounts of campaign contributions, and allow the parties to draw $75,000 from an election fund established in the Commonwealth Treasury.

subsidy measure into law. Subsidies of some kind have been favored by many of the leading students of party finance.[37]

Senator Neuberger's is the most thoroughgoing recent proposal of this sort. Were his plan enacted, the federal government would give a sizable subsidy to the national committee of each major party to support the campaigns of candidates for federal office.[38] It would require, as a condition for receipt of the subsidy, a certification by the officers of each of the national committees "that no individual has contributed more than a total of $100 to the campaign of one or more candidates for Federal office" of that committee's party.[39] The plan would define as a "major party," any political party that had polled at least 10 per cent of the total popular vote for its presidential candidate in the preceding election or had polled the same proportion of the total popular vote for its senatorial and congressional candidates.

On behalf of his bill Senator Neuberger argued that subsidies would discourage fraud in elections, lessen the dependence of candidates on "shady" or interested contributions, and equalize the access of candidates to the media of communication.[40] Without prejudice to these arguments, it should

[37] James K. Pollock, Louise Overacker, Alexander Heard, Clarence Berdahl, Hugh Bone, and Ralph M. Goldman have all gone on record as favoring subsidies. See *Campaign Contributions, Political Activities and Lobbying,* Hearings before the Senate Special Committee to Investigate Political Activities, Lobbying, and Campaign Contributions, 84 Cong. 2 sess., pp. 1268-86.

[38] "Payments authorized by this Act shall be made to the national committee of each major political party in a total amount for each such committee in any two-year period, beginning April 1 following a national election—if during that two-year period presidential electors are to be elected, not to exceed the amount obtained by multiplying 20 cents by the average total number of voters casting votes for candidates for the offices of presidential elector and Delegate to Congress in the last two elections for those offices; and if during that two-year period presidential electors are not to be elected, not to exceed the amount obtained by multiplying 15 cents by the average total number of votes cast for all candidates for Representative and Delegate, in the last two nonpresidential elections." S. 3242, 84 Cong. 2 sess.

[39] *Ibid.*

[40] Richard L. Neuberger, "Federal Funds for Party Coffers," *The Christian Century* (Jan. 25, 1956), pp. 105-07.

be noted also that the particular plan for subsidies that the Senator offered would radically alter the character of American political parties. The present decentralization of power in the two major parties is accompanied and supported by a decentralized system of party finance. The Neuberger proposal, by transferring control of campaign funds from local party groups to the two national committees, would have a powerful centralizing effect on the direction of all other party activities. To assess the plan's advantages and disadvantages fully, therefore, would be beyond the scope of the present study.

Subsidies could be given directly to major party candidates for specific purposes, however, without significantly affecting present candidate-party relationships. Three proposals that involve this type of campaign subsidization are those for a wider use of voters' pamphlets, the granting of a limited franking privilege to nonincumbent candidates, and the giving of government grants for radio and television time. Workable plans for carrying out the first two should be easy to develop. A subsidy for radio and television time would require some practicable procedure for allocating time and determining a candidate's eligibility for the grant, but finding such a procedure is not an impossible task. The problems raised are parallel to those involved in defining claims and eligibility under Section 315, and are amenable to the same sort of solution.[41]

Limited subsidies of the type just discussed would help to ensure all serious candidates of the two major parties a minimum opportunity to communicate their qualifications and views to the public. They are administratively feasible and would work no "unwanted revolution in our political party

[41] See pp. 44-45 above.

organization."[42] Though there are refinements of limited subsidy plans that merit consideration, such plans are a basically sound approach to a serious problem of government.

Summary

A few words will suffice to sum up the discussion thus far: If campaign discussion is to encourage rationality in voting, rival candidates must enjoy comparable access to the attention of voters—they must reach the same audience or audiences—and they must keep the attention of voters long enough to state the essential elements of their respective cases. Available evidence would indicate that both these objectives are imperfectly realized in contemporary campaigns. The campaign audiences for rival candidates tend to be separate audiences, and the audiences for both candidates tend to have a shifting and changing membership.

Several factors seem to contribute to this state of affairs—a tendency for voters to seek propaganda consistent with their partisan preferences and to ignore all other campaign discussion; a tendency of parties and candidates to use propaganda to mobilize the partisan sympathies of their followers and to forego efforts to convert opposition followers; and inadequate and unequal opportunities for campaigners to communicate their views to the electorate. About the first of these factors little can be done, but something can be done to enlarge the opportunities of campaigners to communicate and to reduce the chances for inequalities in their opportunities to communicate. A revision of Section 315 of the Federal Communications Act to make its equal time provisions applicable only

[42] Two requirements Alexander Heard has set for a campaign subsidy plan. See *Campaign Contributions, Political Activities and Lobbying*, Hearings, 84 Cong. 2 sess, p. 1274.

to major parties and leading candidates would be one step in this direction, as would limited government subsidies to candidates for radio and television time, extension of the franking privilege to candidates, and more extensive use of voters' pamphlets. Something can also be done to change the character of the content of campaign discussion—but that is the subject of the next chapter.

4

Policy Discussion

IF IT IS OBVIOUS that rational electoral decisions presuppose the ability of rival parties and candidates to make their views known, it should be equally obvious that what voters hear is at least as important as whether they hear. Discussion—as anyone who has participated in it well knows—may obscure as well as illuminate the grounds for rational choice, may favor nonrational as well as rational behavior. No assessment of the value of discussion in campaigns, therefore, can fail to take into account the way in which politicians shape and mold its content.

This conclusion is apt to be somewhat disturbing to the reformer, for if the content of campaign discussion is weighed and found wanting, no remedial action readily suggests itself. Given the constitutional protection of free speech and publication, it is clear that no authority exists for enforcing any particular pattern of communication on campaigners; one that contributes to rational electoral decisions must somehow develop naturally out of the competition of parties and candidates for electoral support. The democrat and civil libertarian is tempted, therefore, to dismiss any further consideration of what is a potentially serious flaw in his political philosophy by assuming campaign discussion to be valuable, whatever form it may take. Not to do so would be an apparent capitulation to those who have argued that free discussion of public issues can in practice be either an evil or worthless.

In fact, however, he is faced with a problem, not a dilemma. Anyone who examines the course of discussion in campaigns can hardly fail to conclude that it is often as well designed to subvert as to facilitate rational voting behavior. What candidates say frequently lacks relevance to any decision voters face, exposes differences in the views of candidates imperfectly, and is filled with evasions, ambiguities, and distortions. But campaign communication is not all of a piece. Its content varies with the form campaigning takes, a fact that has important implications for those who would like to see a change in its character. It is the purpose of the present chapter, therefore, to analyze in detail this relationship between form and content in campaigning, particularly as it affects the discussion of policy issues.

Policy Issues In Campaign Speeches, 1956

This analysis can appropriately begin by examining the way policy questions were treated in the candidates' speeches in the presidential campaign of 1956. Of all the policy pronouncements made in the course of campaigning, those made by the candidates are given the most serious attention by the electorate and are regarded as most responsible. Where political parties show as little discipline in policy matters as they do in the United States, it could hardly be otherwise. The policy statements made by the candidates in 1956 cannot, of course, necessarily be taken as representative of those in all campaigns, but their choice for the purpose of illustrating the way candidates deal with issues is at least a defensible one. There was little that was bitter and almost nothing that could be called scurrilous in the second Eisenhower-Stevenson race for the Presidency. On the contrary, it was at the time remarked upon as unusually "high level." An analysis of the quality of campaign discussion based on it, therefore, is unlikely to lead to unnecessarily pessimistic or alarmist conclusions.

Nonetheless, to measure policy discussion as it was carried on in the Eisenhower-Stevenson speeches against an ideal standard is not reassuring. Much of the time, both candidates described their policy positions in terms so general that their statements lacked any clear relation to issues on which voters had to make decisions. Both were for peace, social welfare, full justice for farmers, honest government, a strong national defense, the expansion of civil liberties, full employment, the development of individual talents, a vigorous economy, a flourishing world trade, and a large number of other objectives of similarly general appeal. They voiced their allegiance to these ideals again and again. Sometimes they did so in slightly different words, and sometimes one mentioned goals that were not mentioned by the other, but at no time did either candidate declare himself to be opposed to any statement of fundamental belief that his opponent had advanced. This kind of expression by candidates of their basic policy objectives has a place in campaign discussion, for voters need to know if they differ in this respect. At the point it becomes clear that they do not, however—and this point was reached rather early in the 1956 campaign—such discussion of fundamentals ceases to have revelance to the voter's choice.

Indeed, the two candidates enunciated clearly defined pro and con positions on only a few policy issues in the course of the entire campaign. Farm policy was one of these. Governor Stevenson advocated government support for basic farm commodities at 90 per cent of parity. President Eisenhower opposed guaranteed price supports at that level. Policy on H-bomb testing was another. Stevenson said that the American government should initiate action to bring an end to hydrogen bomb tests. Eisenhower said that it should not. The latter issue was perhaps the best discussed of the campaign. While the statements of the two candidates on farm policy had a more or less static character—they simply stated and repeated what they apparently believed to be their best arguments—their discussion of H-bomb testing showed a kind of progression. As it continued, they defined their positions more and more carefully, clarified their differences, and began to subject each other's reasoning to criticism.

Governor Stevenson, who had previously spoken on the subject of H-bomb testing, introduced it into the 1956 campaign in his address to the American Legion Convention in Los Angeles. He regretted the fact, he told Legion members on that occasion, that his proposal to "halt further testing of large nuclear devices . . . conditioned upon adherence to a similar policy by other atomic powers,"[1] had been so casually dismissed by the administration. He left the matter stand at this, however, until the President termed his statement, some time later, a "theatrical gesture." Then the press reported in mid-October that Stevenson had decided to give the issue major emphasis.

This decision taken, Stevenson defined his proposal with more precision. He now said that he favored a halt on all further tests by any nation of larger-sized nuclear weapons and advocated that the United States take the lead in establishing this world policy. He would not go further than this. His proposal implied no halt in the production of nuclear weapons and no reduction of nuclear weapon stockpiles. It did not mean that the United States should abandon tests of smaller nuclear weapons. It did not mean that the United States should halt preparation for H-bomb tests.

Having stated his position, Stevenson began also to state the reasons that, in his view, favored its adoption. He contended

[1] *New York Times*, Sept. 7, 1956.

that a moratorium on further testing would: (1) leave the United States superior to the Russians in atomic technology; (2) prevent the spread of H-bomb technology to nations other than Russia, Great Britain, and the United States; (3) win the respect of neutralist or uncommitted nations; (4) break the United States–Soviet Union stalemate in negotiations on disarmament; and (5) diminish air pollution from radioactive fallout and the dangers fallout involved for health and heredity. The proposal was a practical one, said Stevenson, because an agreement to stop tests would be self-enforcing. H-bomb explosions violating the agreement would be detectable without inspection.

President Eisenhower at first appeared intent on avoiding involvement in controversy. On September 19 he told a campaign audience that: "We cannot prove wise and strong by any such simple device as suspending, unilaterally, our H-bomb tests."[2] In his press conference on October 12, he advised reporters that he had said his last words on the matter.

But this decision did not stand. In later statements the President gave reasons for rejecting Stevenson's proposal. In the first place, he argued, stopping the tests was less important than stopping the use of nuclear weapons in a war, and this latter objective could be accomplished only as a part of a general disarmament agreement. Secondly, the Soviet superiority in man power meant that the United States must at all costs preserve its superiority in nuclear weapons. Since tests require long preparation, the United States could fall far behind the Russians in nuclear research by the time an explosion was detected, if it should halt its tests and test preparations. Thirdly, the danger to health from radioactive fallout attending the tests was not serious. He cited a report of the National Academy of Science in support of this conten-

[2] *Public Papers of the Presidents of the United States, Dwight D. Eisenhower, 1956,* p. 786.

54

tion. Fourthly, further tests would allow progress toward a "clean" bomb, that is, one creating less fallout. Finally, the assumption that all tests could be detected by monitoring was unverified.

This analysis of the course the argument took could be carried further, for each of the candidates suggested new evidence for his contentions as these were subjected to criticism by his opponent. It has been carried far enough, however, to show that policy issues can sometimes be discussed in campaigns with reasonable clarity. Stevenson's introduction of the issue of H-bomb testing into the campaign may have been—probably was—politically inexpedient, since the matter had been given little public attention beforehand. It is the form the discussion took that is under consideration here, however, and it should be evident that, in this instance, discussion both defined a choice for voters and gave them a great deal of information useful in choosing.

This last judgment must be qualified somewhat, because the H-bomb issue was in reality discussed on two quite different levels. The arguments summarized above are drawn from a few of Stevenson's speeches, a memorandum he prepared, a memorandum released by the White House, and some of President Eisenhower's statements in press conferences. In many of their campaign addresses, however, both candidates presented their cases in a quite different fashion—the speeches of one candidate seemed often not so much to reflect the content of his rival's as to refract it. In answer to Stevenson's statement that he wanted to suspend testing "conditioned upon adherence by other atomic powers," President Eisenhower derided the idea of stopping our testing program unilaterally. Both candidates relied heavily on unsupported assertion in their treatment of the subject, and frequently ignored opposition reasoning.

It has already been noted that discussion defining issues as clearly as that which centered on H-bomb testing was rare in the 1956 campaign. More often, points on which differences in the policy views of the two candidates might have been clarified never were, because one or the other failed to take any notice of what his opponent was saying. At different times Governor Stevenson criticized the Eisenhower foreign-aid program as putting too much emphasis on military aid, and too little emphasis on economic aid. He attacked the administration's handling of the security investigations of federal employees. He called the President's defense strategy an "all or nothing" policy, implying an improper balance of defense expenditures. He attacked the administration's information policy. There is no reason to believe that the policies he had questioned were not susceptible to discussion or that such discussion might not have contributed to public understanding of the reasons such policies had been undertaken. In none of these cases, however, did President Eisenhower acknowledge that there had been any questioning. Candidates act as people professing hardness of hearing sometimes do. They hear what they want to hear, whether it is shouted or whispered.

President Eisenhower's silence was not without advantage to his cause. By not answering these criticisms, he avoided giving them added publicity. The President's failure to answer was also in some ways helpful to Governor Stevenson. He could capitalize on dissatisfaction attending the governmental actions he criticized without having to specify what he would do, or would have done, differently. Failure to answer meant that both candidates, however, could leave their positions in these areas essentially ambiguous. And they did.

Nor is this the only way in which ambiguity enters policy discussion in campaigns. The draft controversy is one of the best examples that 1956 provides of an issue that, while hotly disputed by both sides, never drew any clear line of difference between them. Governor Stevenson initiated the dispute in his address to the American Legion. As he developed it subsequently, Stevenson's position on the draft can be fairly stated as follows: Military thinkers foresee a need for a preponderance of highly professional units in the defense forces of the future. While an immediate end to the draft may not be feasible, changes in military technology "may well mean that we will need and want in the foreseeable future to turn to a method other than the draft" to recruit military personnel.[3] Thus, there should be a "fresh look" at the military manpower situation, for it might well indicate that the burdens of the draft on the nation's youth could be avoided and American defenses strengthened at one and the same time.

Questioned in press conference, President Eisenhower said that he saw no chance to end the draft in the immediate future. In his view, an end to the draft "under world conditions of today" would weaken American defense forces, encourage neutralist sentiment abroad, and discourage allies whom the United States was trying to get to maintain their own draft armies. All this meant continuance of the draft for the immediate future, although "every family naturally hopes for the day when it might be possible" to end compulsory conscription.[4]

As the campaign drew to a close, talk about the draft became more and more compressed into two contrasting themes. Governor Stevenson appealed to a hope that the draft could be ended and accused his opponent of "negativism." President Eisenhower held it to be against common sense to think that a stronger defense and an end to the draft were compatible aims. The volume and intensity of the words that were poured into propagating these appeals should not obscure the fact that

[3] Address delivered October 18, 1956. See Adlai E. Stevenson, *The New America* (1957), p. 61.

[4] Address delivered September 19, 1956. See *Public Papers . . . Dwight D. Eisenhower, 1956*, p. 786.

the issue was never really joined. The disagreement—if there really was one—would appear to have been about when and under what conditions the draft could be ended. Yet nothing was said by either candidate that would not have permitted him with consistency and political decorum to (1) ask for an end of the draft, or (2) not ask for an end to the draft, in the period 1956-1960. Some deductions about the motives and characters of the candidates, but little notion of their differences on draft policy, may be possible from an observation of their conduct during this dispute.

This kind of ambiguity in the policy views of the two candidates was frequently complicated further by distortion. A voter who had asked their help in piecing together an account of the nation's recent political history, as one would fit together a jig-saw puzzle, might easily have quit his task in frustration and hopeless confusion. Each would have offered him pieces apparently destined for the same place in the puzzle, yet of entirely different shapes and colors. When the voter asked for other pieces needed to fill quite obvious gaps, he would have found that neither had any suggestion regarding where he might find them.

The needs of the nation's schools were, for example, one of the subjects most thoroughly discussed by both candidates in 1956. Both advocated federal aid to education. President Eisenhower told voters that his program for school aid had been rejected by the opposition in Congress and promised to ask the new Congress for legislation that would make up for the lost time.[5] Governor Stevenson charged that the President had failed to take any decisive action to meet school problems in his first term of office and that "the Republicans in Congress defeated a bill for federal aid to education."[6]

Thus the Eisenhower and Stevenson speeches succeeded in

[5] Address delivered October 9, 1956. See *ibid.*, p. 874.
[6] *New York Times*, Sept. 23, 1956.

giving conflicting accounts of the congressional battle over aid to education, while they left the voter largely ignorant about what had actually happened. The statements each made were technically true, but what they said was less important for a realistic understanding of the school issue than what they did not say. The school program proposed by the Eisenhower administration and the Democratic program that "the Republicans in Congress defeated" differed significantly in only one respect—the formula by which funds were to be distributed to the states. The speeches of neither candidate gave any hint of this, nor of the fact that this difference had been largely compromised by the time the school bill came up for a final vote. They said nothing, moreover, of the crucial role played in the whole controversy by the Powell amendment, which would have denied funds to states maintaining segregated school systems. President Eisenhower had opposed this amendment, as had Southern Democrats. Many Northern Democrats had supported it, although doing so meant almost certain defeat for the school aid bill, and ninety-six Republicans in the House of Representatives had voted for it, but against the school bill as amended. But none of this could have been learned from the Eisenhower-Stevenson discussion of the issue.

It would not be too extreme to say that distortion was so integral a part of the cases presented by the two candidates in the 1956 campaign, that the campaign was in large part repetitious assertion of fictitious "issues." Each of the candidates reserved some of his most biting phrases for attacks on positions his opponent had never taken. Governor Stevenson, for example, again and again characterized the Republicans as complacent, fatuously complacent, fatuously optimistic, negative, smug, and self-righteous, insensitive to human problems, and purveyors of Pollyana politics. On one occasion, he observed that "the political lines in this country are now sharply drawn between those who are satisfied with things exactly as they are and those who feel, on the other hand, that there is still a tremendous lot to be done in America and in the world."[7] Presumably he had not heard President Eisenhower say, as he did in one speech, "Our task is far from done. New problems, and critical ones, rise before us."[8] Nor that "There will never be room for boasting . . . until there is not a single needy person left in the United States, when distress and disease have been eliminated."[9]

This is not to say that Stevenson's views were represented with any greater accuracy. The Democratic candidate, as leader of the opposition, naturally pointed to unsolved problems, but he also said, "We are told that America is prosperous. And it is—in part. We are thankful and we are proud."[10] President Eisenhower, however, professed to have heard the Democrats tell voters "you are not prosperous, you are starving —you are poor—we are not working."[11] And he often characterized the men to whom he had gratuitously attributed these words as "wailing politicians" who were painting, for partisan purposes, a false picture of gloom and doom.

What happened in the Eisenhower-Stevenson discussion of policy issues may be summed up at this point. Each candidate defined his position in terms so general that it became almost impossible to distinguish it from that of his opponent. Moderate differences that in fact charcterized the two candidates' policy orientations were misrepresented or ignored. Each of them instead argued the virtues of his self-defined modcrate program versus an extreme and largely fictitious one that he

[7] Address delivered October 18, 1956. See Stevenson, *The New America*, p. 59.
[8] Address delivered September 19, 1956. See *Public Papers . . . Dwight D. Eisenhower, 1956*, p. 784.
[9] Address delivered October 1, 1956. See *ibid.*, p. 832.
[10] *New York Times*, Sept. 4, 1956.
[11] Address delivered October 29, 1956. See *Public Papers . . . Dwight D. Eisenhower, 1956*, p. 1056.

attributed to his opponent. Campaign discussion of policy questions was not one in which issues and differences were mutually acknowledged and defined. Rather it involved the independent and systematic propagation of competing notions of what the differences and issues were.

Policy discussion may not assume this pattern in all campaign speeches, but it undoubtedly does so very often. Lazarsfeld, Berelson, and their colleagues found a similar one in comprehensive analyses of campaign propaganda in the presidential campaigns of 1940 and 1948. In those campaigns, each side attacked its opponent's record much more often than it defended its own. Both "tended to 'talk past each other,' almost as though they were participating in two different elections."[12] Both devoted a great deal of time to discussing vaguely phrased goals, and little to specifying the methods by which such goals were to be realized. But the pattern has been best described, perhaps, by James Bryce:

> The object of each party naturally is to put forward as many good political issues as it can, claiming for itself the merit of having always been on the popular side. Any one who should read the campaign literature of the Republicans would fancy that they were opposed to the Democrats on many important points. When he took up the Democratic speeches and pamphlets he would be again struck by the serious divergences between the parties, which however would seem to arise, not on the points raised by the Republicans, but on other points which the Republicans had not referred to. In other words, the aim of each party is to force on its antagonist certain issues which the antagonist rarely accepts, so that although there is a vast deal of discussion and declamation on political topics, there are few on which either party directly traverses the doctrines of the other. Each pummels, not his true enemy, but a stuffed figure set up to represent that enemy.[13]

[12] Bernard Berelson, Paul F. Lazarsfeld, and William N. McPhee, *Voting* (1954), p. 236.
[13] James Bryce, *The American Commonwealth* (1890), Vol. II, p. 208.

Campaign Discussion: Form and Substance

Because the speeches of the candidates are so central to campaign discussion, they tend to set the tone for campaign discussion in its entirety, leaving as the dominant impression in the observer's mind a peculiar pattern of both avoidance and manufacture of issues. That impression can easily be misleading, for the pattern is not an all-pervading one. In the 1956 campaign, for example, the issue of H-bomb testing was discussed somewhat differently than were other policy questions, although not so differently in the speeches as in other forms of communication. This latter fact suggests, if but faintly, that there may be a general relation between the medium used to distribute campaign appeals and the nature of the appeal distributed—that form affects substance. This relationship was also suggested by the analysis of debates in an earlier chapter, and the more one examines the way in which policy discussion is carried on in different media and in different situations, the stronger the suggestion becomes.

Policy discussion through radio and television spot announcements, for example, reflects the same basic tendencies present in campaign speeches, but exaggerates them to a point bordering on the grotesque. A brief analysis of a one spot announcement used by the Republicans in 1952 will illustrate this fact. Its text was as follows:

> Voice: Mr. Eisenhower, what about the high cost of living?
> Eisenhower: My wife, Mamie, worries about the same thing. I tell her it's our job to change that on November 4.

The information contained in these two sentences can be quickly summarized: General Eisenhower and his wife are aware that prices are high. They are concerned about the fact. The General, if elected, proposes to do something about it.

Though the statements of policy intentions in candidates' speeches are often highly ambiguous, ambiguity could hardly be greater than it is here. The announcement gives no notion at all of what kind of action Mr. Eisenhower might take, what the advantages and disadvantages might be of any measures he had in mind, why he would favor these measures over others. The advertising agency that had prepared the spot meant it to show only the General's "complete comprehension" of a problem and "his determination to do something about it when elected." He would thus inspire loyalty "without prematurely committing himself to any strait-jacketing answer."[14]

Nor could any statement have disregarded opposition arguments more completely. Standing alone as it does, it suggests that General Eisenhower must make a point of his concern about high living costs because his opponent is not similarly concerned. To appreciate the fact that it does carry such an implication, one need only consider how greatly the persuasive impact of the announcement would have been reduced, had it given any indication that Governor Stevenson was also expressing his determination to do something about the evils of inflation. In spot announcements, the tendency of candidates to talk past each other reaches an extreme.

General statements about the treatment of policy issues in campaign literature are of more limited applicability than those about policy discussion either in campaign speeches or in spot announcements. Considering the body of literature that was distributed in 1956 as a whole, one would conclude that discussion of policy problems in it closely paralleled that in the candidate's speeches. Both sides pointed with pride to their past accomplishments without describing those accomplishments very accurately or in much detail. They pledged

[14] Quoted in Stanley Kelley, Jr., *Professional Public Relations and Political Power* (1956), p. 188.

themselves to resolve problems but failed to say how they would do so. Issues were often greatly oversimplified, history frequently misread, and statistics misused. This conclusion, however, obscures some significant deviations from this pattern in particular items of the literature. Policy discussion in the booklets, pamphlets, memoranda, leaflets, and post cards of the two parties was presented on at least two different levels.

In many instances, the appeals made were similar in character to those in spot announcements. A Republican comic book, for example, advised that, "More people are employed today than ever before! There are 4,000,000 more jobs now in PEACE TIME than the Democrats had with their WARS!"[15] Two Democratic "score cards" stated in an equally bald fashion that the Republicans had "failed to do anything about over-crowded schools"[16] and had "tried to prevent" a one dollar minimum wage.[17] If the first statement is not to be put down as simply untrue, then it must be construed in a way that would make it equally valid to say that the Democrats had "done nothing" about the school problem. The second statement also suggests a conclusion unwarranted by the facts of the minimum wage dispute. President Eisenhower had indeed opposed a one dollar minimum wage, but he had been for raising the minimum wage to ninety cents.

There were other cases, however, where the campaign literature distributed in 1956 went further than the speeches in clarifying policy issues and the problems out of which they arose. This could be said of a number of the memoranda on policy questions prepared by Adlai Stevenson, and, on the Republican side, of Secretary Ezra T. Benson's pamphlet article,

[15] Republican National, Congressional, and Senatorial Committees, *Forward with Eisenhower-Nixon.*
[16] *What the G.O.P. Has Done to Joe Smith.*
[17] *Pocket Score Card, What the GOPs Did to You!*

"Farmers at the Crossroads." The authors of these pieces attempted to show in detail the causes of the problems they discussed, to suggest remedies for them, to contrast these remedies with those advocated by the other side, and to justify the policy positions they advanced.

Campaign discussion as it occurred in the press conferences of the candidates followed a course still less like that which developed in the speeches. Under questioning by members of the press, Eisenhower and Stevenson modified considerably some of the themes on which they played in other propaganda. They found it more difficult to evade particular subjects and less easy to state their positions ambiguously. They found it necessary to address themselves to arguments made by the opposition and to accept or reject responsibility for what their supporters were saying.

The so-called "tight money" policy of the Eisenhower administration, for example, was subjected to continued and vigorous attack throughout the 1956 campaign by Adlai Stevenson, who said it meant higher interest rates for farmers, small businessmen, and home builders. The strength of his attack seemed to indicate that he meant to do something about tight money if elected, and therefore raised questions about the relationship he meant to establish with the Federal Reserve System. The answers to these questions cannot be found in his speeches, but in a press conference he made it clear that he would ask for no change in the formal position of independence of the System. "Would you, if elected," a reporter of the Buffalo *Evening News* asked the Governor, "support and continue an independent Federal Reserve System and, particularly, the independence of the Federal Reserve System's Open Market Committee?" Stevenson's answer was "I would make, on the basis of what information I have with respect to the working of the Federal Reserve System, I would suggest no legislation to alter the present position of the Federal Reserve System with respect to the Treasury Department and also with respect to its Open Market Committee."[18]

President Eisenhower's responses to questions from the press also qualified the meaning of statements he had made in campaign addresses. In one speech the President posed this question to his audience: "What do we want this country to be like as the next four years unfold?"[19] Part of the picture of America he himself constantly kept before him, he said, was "An America where the greatest possible government efficiency allows the lowest possible government costs—and, hence, lower taxes."[20] When a reporter asked the President in his next press conference to specify how soon such tax cuts might be expected, however, his answer made the prospect for lower taxes seem considerably less hopeful than it might have appeared to the audience for his speech. The chances for tax reduction were not "bright or something right around the corner." Efficiency in government would open up "the avenue by which tax reductions will properly be some day accomplished," but the President did not mean, he said, that they would come "right away, not at all."[21]

It was in a press conference, too, that the President declined to endorse a line of argument that was being pursued by the Republican National, senatorial, and congressional committees. This was their comic book charge, already noted, that identified past wars with the Democratic party. Would the President, asked a reporter of the Louisville *Courier-Journal,* agree that here had been Democratic wars? President Eisenhower's slightly embarrassed answer was: "They may be thinking of something I don't know anything about, but I

[18] *New York Times,* Sept. 18, 1956.
[19] Address delivered October 1, 1956. See *Public Papers . . . Dwight D. Eisenhower, 1956,* p. 840.
[20] *Ibid.,* p. 841.
[21] *Ibid.,* p. 858.

don't believe when America gets into war we can afford to call it anything but our war."[22]

These few examples of the way issues are treated in press conferences are not, of course, meant to show that press conferences at present have any substantial impact on the character of campaign discussion considered in its entirety. Their impact is relatively slight for at least two reasons. In the first place, although they allow questioning, they rarely involve cross questioning. A subject of inquiry may be opened but often cannot be pursued very far. Secondly, candidates tend to grant few press conferences. In 1956 President Eisenhower did continue the regular presidential press conference into the campaign period, meeting the press six times, but Adlai Stevenson, after his nomination, held only two press conferences not limited as to subject matter. In the 1952 campaign, Stevenson held only one press conference, Eisenhower none. What is of interest here, however, is that an examination of the texts of candidate press conferences reveals a different kind of discussion than that found in the speeches.

Something happens also, as has already been argued, when policy discussion involves face-to-face debates between candidates. It is not possible to illustrate this fact by comparing the treatment of issues in the 1956 Eisenhower-Stevenson speeches, with their treatment in an Eisenhower-Stevenson debate, since, of course, none occurred. Comparing policy discussion in two debates of the 1956 New York senatorial race with that in the Eisenhower-Stevenson speeches, however, may give some indication of the way such discussion is modified in the debating situation. Such a comparison, though not ideal for the purposes of the present analysis, provides a reasonably satisfactory basis for it. The New York senatorial candidates (Jacob Javits, then Attorney-General of New York State, and Mayor Robert Wagner) held policy views substantially like

[22] *Ibid.*, p. 811.

those of their respective parties' presidential aspirants, particularly on the two issues they met to debate—civil rights and foreign policy.

There was a striking difference in the treatment of the civil rights question in the two cases. Eisenhower and Stevenson emphasized and re-emphasized their general concern with the problems of minorities and their general desire to see minorities win their full legal rights. They said little about any specific programs for dealing with civil rights problems. Wagner and Javits, though each affirmed his belief in equality, devoted the greater part of their opening speeches to stating in quite specific terms what they would do about civil rights questions when confronted with them in the Senate.

The records and policy stands of the two parties were less distorted in the Javits-Wagner debates than they were in the Eisenhower-Stevenson speeches. It could easily seem incredible to anyone not familiar with American campaigning to learn that neither Eisenhower nor Stevenson ever gave more than the barest hint that their respective parties were not completely united in their approaches to civil rights problems. But they did not; Stevenson constantly referred to the "Democratic" stand on civil rights, Eisenhower to the "Republican" stand. Javits and Wagner made no attempt to maintain the fiction of united parties. Their discussion proceeded, therefore, on a considerably more realistic basis.

Apparently, Javits and Wagner also found it more difficult to avoid taking positions on policy questions than did the two presidential candidates. In the foreign policy debate, for instance, Javits chided Wagner for maintaining silence on Stevenson's proposals for suspending H-bomb tests, and the Mayor felt obliged, after the debate, to issue a statement indicating his support of Mr. Stevenson. In the civil rights debate, Mayor Wagner took advantage of the debating situation to use a tactic that most probably would have fallen on deaf ears had it been used in other circumstances. In his opening speech, the Mayor made a promise and issued a challenge:

> I expect as a newly elected member of the Senate to be on the floor of the Senate on January 3rd to make the motion to change the rules so that civil rights legislation can be readily enacted. That will be a crucial motion. I make this challenge to my opponent. My opponent, even if elected to the Senate, cannot be there to take his oath and support the move against the filibuster. I now invite him to explain why he could not be in the Senate on January 3rd to help in this crucial fight, and why he has surrendered, in advance, his obligation to join in this struggle. If he doesn't answer this question I will give the answer later in the course of this debate.[23]

It is almost needless to add that Javits did attempt an explanation.[24]

The effect of the debating situation on policy discussion in this instance, then, supports the general conclusions about those effects reached before: It led the candidates to state their positions with greater clarity and in more specific terms. It led each to acknowledge the other's position. It reduced distortion in accounts of party records and party policies.

As a final point in this analysis of form and substance in campaign communication, it should be noted that policy discussion may be variously transformed when it is presented as news. This is a fact of considerable significance in making any over-all assessment of the character of campaign discussion,

[23] *New York Times*, Oct. 21, 1956.

[24] Javits' difficulties grew out of the following situation: When a vacancy occurs in the office of the Attorney General of New York, a successor is elected by the State Legislature if it is in session or appointed by the Governor if it is not. Since the Republican controlled Legislature, which could be expected to choose a Republican to succeed Javits, did not convene until after the opening session of Congress, Javits could not be sworn in as a senator at that session without allowing Democratic Governor Averell Harriman to fill his former office with a Democrat. Javits, in his reply to Wagner's question, explained his predicament to the debate audience and promised that if Harriman would pledge himself to make no appointment before the Legislature met, he, Javits, would resign his office and attend the opening session of Congress.

since much of it comes to the public only as it has been selected for, and reflected in, the news and editorial comment of newspapers, magazines, radio, and television. News presentation is not uniform for the press as a whole, but some of the ways it can shape communication between politicians and the electorate can be outlined here.

The press can, for example, help reduce distortion in campaign discussion. Editors can show half-truths for what they are by noting inaccuracies or supplying missing information in reporting a candidate's version of political history or of his opponent's views. If they follow such a policy consistently, they may not only lessen the consequences of distortion but the campaigner's temptation to distort as well. A selective presentation of facts is a useful tactic in persuasion only when those whom one is trying to persuade are not aware that there has been selection.

The press may also make it less difficult for voters to compare the policy positions taken by candidates. Reasonably full and equal coverage of campaign activities is one obvious method by which it can do so. Several tricks of display are another: shared headlines; boxes that refer the reader to opposition speeches or to other news bearing on some point made by a candidate; and, when one candidate refers to a statement of his opponent, the bracketing in of relevant material. Nor is this all. Campaign statements as they are issued by candidates do not lend themselves nicely to running comparisons. At any one time, rival candidates are most often talking about quite different subjects. Such discontinuities are at least partially remedied by weekly summaries of the campaign and feature articles that give detailed accounts of what candidates have said or not said on particular issues of public policy.

Finally, the press can encourage campaigners to debate. Radio and television have done so by organizing face-to-face debates and forums, although usually these do not involve candidates. A device newspapers have used is the so-called "battle page," a page where rival candidates or party committees are given an opportunity to argue their cases in adjoining columns. These efforts have not been uniformly successful—newspaper editors in particular have mixed feelings about the value of the battle page feature. They complain that copy submitted to them is often vague, platitudinous, and dull; that party committees frequently miss the newspaper's deadline; and that the committees delegate the task of writing battle page copy to anonymous press agents. On occasion, however, the battle page has been a highly successful feature. Candidates have begun to issue and answer challenges, and, when such has been the case, reader interest has been high.

Why do candidates sometimes take and sometimes fail to take the opportunity to debate what the battle page affords them? Willingness to debate undoubtedly depends in part on the size of the audience the newspaper offers them. Moreover, the usual practice of allocating battle page space to party committees rather than directly to candidates probably discourages debate, for, given the present organization of our political parties, there are few such committees that can really presume to speak for the men on their parties' tickets. The editorial initiative taken by the newspaper is probably important also. The Santa Fe *New Mexican,* for example, decreased the number of deadlines missed by enlisting the support of the League of Women Voters for its battle page project. And the rules set up for the battle page may make a considerable difference. The *Toledo Blade* found that its battle page made better copy once the editor began to require partisan contributors to address themselves to the same general topic on the same day.

It may be useful at this point to summarize the foregoing

analysis of variations in the content and character of campaign discussion. Examination of policy discussion in most campaign speeches, spot announcements, and campaign literature discloses most of the shortcomings that have led critics to conclude that campaign discussion can contribute little to the rationality of electoral decisions. When such discussion is examined as it occurs in other forms of electioneering, these shortcomings are not present to the same extent. The pattern that dominates most campaign discussion, then—a pattern in which campaigners avoid or distort differences in their views that are moderate but actual, and create fictitious issues to replace real ones—cannot be put down as an inevitable result of the campaign situation, and certain common explanations of this pattern must be regarded as less than satisfactory. The desire of campaigners to maximize votes cannot wholly account for it; presumably, campaigners are attempting to maximize political support in all forms of campaigning. The quality of the electorate cannot explain it adequately, for different forms of campaigning may be aimed at essentially the same electorate. The lack of any issues capable of discussion is not an explanation, for those that are drawn in one form of campaign discussion may be ignored in another.

How can variations in the treatment of issues through different media and in different situations be accounted for? The deliberate policy of those who manage the news media is obviously responsible for some of this variation. The technical capacities and limitations of particular media are also a factor. It is not possible to argue a complex issue in a spot announcement. Nor can a problem be so fully canvassed in a half-hour television speech as it can in a pamphlet or memorandum. An explanation of wider applicability than either of these, however, would be this: The content of campaign communication varies with changes in the relationship between campaigners and between campaigners and their audiences.

The character of discussion in campaign speeches is more understandable if one thinks of speeches as designed for an audience with a highly variable membership that tends to expose itself unequally to the propaganda of opposing sides. Candidates constantly repeat statements of general belief because the membership of their audience shifts and changes. They are in the same position a debater would be, if he were to find that the audience for his opening speech was not the same audience as that for his rebuttal. Each candidate also finds it easy to ignore what his opponent is saying, to avoid answering his opponent's challenges, and to give a distorted account of his opponent's views because he believes himself to be addressing a different audience than that reached by his opponent. To state it another way, candidates in their speeches act as if the audience for their attacks would not hear their opponents' replies, as if the audience for their opponents' criticisms would not hear their own replies, as if the attention of the campaign audience were too casual for it to discern areas of agreement and disagreement, contradictions, and inconsistencies. Thus the existence of a segmented audience and an audience of variable membership is not just an indication that competition in political communication is imperfect; it also changes the character of the communication aimed at voters.

The content of spot announcements would seem to be shaped by the same general considerations as are speeches. Spot announcements are aimed primarily at those whose interest and involvement in campaign discussion are low; that is, they are designed to capture the attention of voters who do not attend on their own initiative. They are also used in an effort to gain a differential access to this kind of audience. The so-called Republican "blitz" campaign in 1952 was, for example, timed to reach voters "at too late a date for effective

Democratic rebuttal."[25] Repetition, ambiguity, distortion, and ignoring of opposition arguments, therefore, reach their height in the spot announcement, for it is meant to define the campaign for voters who, it is hoped, will have minimum exposure to alternative definitions.

The pattern discussion takes varies in different items of the campaign literature, and, once again, differences in the relationship of the campaigner to his audience would seem to account for much of this variation. In general, the shorter the piece and the wider its intended audience, the more ambiguous is its representation of the candidate's position and the more distorted is its version of records and policies. This kind of literature, which takes the form of handbills, cards, and comic books is distributed for the most part by canvassers, either at random or to their own partisans. The more reasoned statements appear in pieces of literature that are designed for opinion leaders or others who are likely to be familiar with the arguments of both sides. Another aspect of campaigner-audience relationship seems to have a bearing on the character of discussion in the campaign literature, namely, the degree of anonymity that surrounds its authorship. But this will be treated more fully in a later chapter.

If it is true that the content of discussion varies with the relationship of campaigners to their audience, one would expect discussion to show the greatest amount of deviation from its normal forms in press conferences and debates, for there the communicator-audience relationship differs radically from that which attends most campaigning. The greatest change in content does occur in these two situations. The pattern of discussion in the Javits-Wagner debates was not like that in most campaign speeches, and the few Eisenhower-Stevenson press conferences helped to clarify their stands on issues.

In the debate, candidates address identical audiences and

[25] Quoted in Kelley, *op. cit.,* p. 188.

each must therefore assume that what he says will be compared with what his opponent says. In the press conference, discussion becomes a dialogue between the candidate and his immediate audience. The candidate is asked to respond to his opponent's criticisms, stated in his opponent's words. He is confronted by his own past statements and is asked to explain their meaning. He is questioned regarding matters he has not seen fit to treat in his campaign speeches. He is asked to indicate agreement or disagreement with statements made by his supporters. These are tests that he normally does not face, because normally his audience cannot talk back. In most forms of campaigning, it is the campaigner who determines the subjects he will discuss and the times and places he will discuss them.

Changing the Character of Policy Discussion

The conclusions reached in the preceding section suggest some of the measures that might be taken to increase the contribution of campaign discussion to the rationality of electoral decisions. The broad strategy should be to channel campaigning into those kinds of discussion situations that support, or tend to support, rational discourse. In practice this would mean seeking to establish debates, press conferences, and forums as campaign institutions. It would also mean asking the press to report campaigns in a manner calculated to stimulate debate, reduce the temptation for politicians to resort to distortion and falsehood, and encourage the electorate to expose themselves to the arguments of both sides.

There would, of course, be obstacles to changes of this kind. Individual politicians cannot alone change, or afford to change, the forms of campaigning, because contemporary campaign techniques do serve partisan objectives, however poorly they may serve an educational function. Similarly, the press may hesitate to use its potential power to change the character of campaign discussion for reasons both political and ideological. In any case, there are economic and technical limits to that power.

The technical and economic limitations on what the press can do to shape campaign discussion are considerable. Only relatively large papers can readily afford to prepare comprehensive features on what candidates have said, issue by issue. Even these, when their editors want to do that kind of story, may find that the reporter who specializes on some suddenly important issue has already been assigned elsewhere. Not all publishers favor so-called depth reporting, but, even when they do, they may find this policy a difficult one to implement. Reporters following in the wake of rapidly moving candidates cannot easily put background material into their reports, and the compelling drive to meet deadlines may prevent editors from doing what reporters have been unable to do.

Whether or not the press will report campaign statements in depth is an issue of considerable importance, since depth reporting is one of the most effective ways to combat distortion, evasion, and ambiguity. Yet depth reporting is not only technically difficult, it is also inconsistent with the operational definition many newsmen have given the notion of objectivity. As an ideal, objectivity implies divorcement of the press's editorial function from its news function, of its attempts to persuade from its recording of events. Those whom Wallace Carroll has called the fundamentalists of the press take this to mean, however, that reporters "should simply get the facts and present them with as much detachment as they can, but should not try to fill in background, interpret or analyze, especially when they are handling an explosive subject."[26]

[26] Wallace Carroll, "The Seven Deadly Virtues," *Michigan Alumnus Quarterly Review* (Aug. 6, 1955), p. 330.

Obviously, commitment to objectivity defined in this manner would make campaign discussion in the press little more than a photographically exact reproduction of campaign discussion as it is shaped by campaigners.

Unfortunately, some publishers have shown little desire to make it anything else. Newspapers are themselves instruments used in the struggle for power; and some publishers are more intent on influencing the outcome of elections than in changing the character of campaign discussion. H. G. Nicholas, noting with concern the lack of debate in the 1952 presidential campaign, has argued that the press has now more than ever a heavy responsibility to "persuade and bully the rival candidates into acknowledging each other's existence" and to force them into "according each other's arguments the dignity of an occasional reply."[27] But American elections, he observes, tend to become free-for-alls, and "since everyone is expected to participate, no one is left to be referee."[28]

The problems that would attend efforts to get politicians to accept press conferences, debates, and forums as normal campaign devices are of a different nature. Individual politicians might suffer if these forms of campaigning became normal, but politicians as a class would not. They would simply play the game according to new rules.

At present, candidates often see press conferences as threats, to be avoided if possible, since, as they face each other in press conference, candidates and reporters have contrary objectives. "The official," Leo Rosten notes, "wants to present the information which will reflect most favor upon him. The newspaperman, motivated by the ancient values of journalism, is interested in precisely that type of news which the official is least eager to reveal."[29] Candidates are not without

<hr>

[27] H. G. Nicholas, "The Long Morning After, V: Afterthoughts from Abroad," *The Reporter* (May 17, 1953), p. 36.

[28] *Ibid.*, p. 32.

[29] Leo Rosten, *The Washington Correspondents* (1937), p. 65.

resources to meet the threat, for able press assistants and a news sense can help them to anticipate and prepare for many questions. Nonetheless, there remains room enough for the unexpected to occur, to make California's Whitaker and Baxter list the "press conference debacle" as one of the tactical errors into which a candidate can most easily fall.[30]

Candidates (or at least one of each pair of candidates) normally see the debating situation as threatening also. As in a press conference, the politician in a debate cannot nicely calculate the appeals he will make and decorously avoid discussion of all other matters. He is deprived, moreover, of any ability to win a differential access to the electorate, since, by its very nature, the debate gives rival candidates equal access. Since it tends to reduce the advantage that a better-known candidate or a better-financed candidate would otherwise enjoy, it is not likely to be entered willingly by candidates who enjoy such advantages.[31]

This brief review of the difficulties involved in attempts to change forms of campaigning shows that such changes will not come automatically, but it does not support the inference that there is no way to change them at all. Action by the press, by legislators, and by citizen groups could do much to encourage a new kind of campaigning.

Newspapers could take action both individually and collectively to promote press conferences as a regular feature of

---

[30] Clem Whitaker and Leone Baxter, "Campaign Blunders Can Change History," *Public Relations Journal* (August 1956), p. 6.

[31] Thus Whitaker and Baxter, in a letter to the county and local chairman of their organization to promote the candidacy of Goodwin Knight for Governor of California in 1954, observe: "What about debates? Our candidate is a master in this field, so we regret to say we will schedule no debates with our opponents. We should not permit the stature of the Governor to be utilized to build audiences for his opposition." Murray Chotiner, in a lecture on the techniques and strategies of political campaigning given at U.C.L.A., was similarly wary of debate. His advice for candidates considering participation in forums was: "Always pick your own subject and your own opponent or just don't consider them."

campaigning. Editorial explanation of the value of the press conference would be one form such action could take. Resolutions of the editors' and publishers' associations would be another. Still another would be publicizing the willingness or unwillingness of individual candidates to submit to questioning, as the *Washington Post and Times Herald* has done in the case of Cabinet officers. Along with such action, experimentation with varying forms of the press conference might be desirable. Press conferences devoted to cross-questioning candidates on their responses to questions submitted in advance might, for instance, be an improvement on present practices and meet some of the objections candidates have to them at the same time.

Press action should also include more analysis and interpretation of campaign materials and the use of all the techniques that tend to relate the statements of rival candidates and parties to each other. The need for interpretive or depth reporting is now widely recognized among influential newspapermen, partly, one would suppose, because the case for it is persuasive. While press fundamentalists have argued that depth reporting can mean biased reporting, it is equally clear that "objective" reporting can lead readers to badly distorted views of the events reported. Indeed, the fundamentalist view of objectivity often leads to news coverage that is more irresponsible than objective: "[When] . . . a reporter has solid evidence that a statement is misleading," asks Wallace Carroll, "should he merely report that statement or should he give the reader the benefit of his additional knowledge?"[32] If he merely reports, he allows the newspaper to be used, not in the public interest or even in its own, but in that of the propagandist. The economic problems involved in presenting more interpretation and more features could be solved for most

[32] Carroll, *op. cit.*, p. 332.

79

papers if the wire services were to furnish them with this kind of material.

Several kinds of measures to stimulate debate in campaigns are available to legislators. They could require a certain number of face-to-face debates between candidates by law. They could make an allowance of time on radio and television, paid for by the government, conditional on its use for debates between candidates. In the voters' pamphlet, discussed in the preceding chapter, they have already provided a medium for partisan argument that has one of the important features of the debating situation—rival candidates enjoy access to the same audience. If such pamphlets were issued several times during the course of a campaign, candidates could not only make a general statement of their positions, as they do now, but they could also challenge their opponents and draw distinctions between their positions and those of their rivals.[33]

Legislators could, in any case, alter provisions of existing law that now discourage the use of the airways for debate, for the present effect of Section 315 of the Federal Communications Act is to do just that. A spokesman for the Columbia Broadcasting System told a Senate committee that the network had found "most attractive" suggestions made in 1952 that it sponsor a number of Eisenhower-Stevenson debates. CBS officials felt unable to push such a project in earnest, however, since Section 315 would have required them "at least to give the same amount of time to each of the other 16 candidates."[34] To avoid this complication, the networks have depended largely on noncandidate party leaders to present partisan points of view in their debates and press interview

[33] This is a proposal made by Louise Overacker in her *Money in Elections* (1932). See pp. 370-71.

[34] Testimony of Richard S. Salant, Vice President of the Columbia Broadcasting System, in *Federal Elections Act of 1955*, Hearings before the Senate Committee on Rules and Administration, 84 Cong. 1 sess., p. 177.

programs. Valuable as these programs may be, they are hardly substitutes for having candidates speak for themselves.[35]

Finally, citizen groups can play an important role in promoting new conceptions of campaigning and in imposing new practices on campaigners. Normally, candidates, not voters, determine the procedures of campaign discussion, but this need not always be so. Voters can turn the tables on politicians if they organize themselves to exact conditions for continuing to listen. A number of citizen groups in various localities have done something very like this and have done it successfully. The voters' service program of the League of Women Voters offers a good example of such action, and one which might well be emulated by other civic groups.

Local League groups carry on several types of activity that contribute to, and condition, campaign discussion. One of the most widespread is the submission of questionnaires to candidates and the publication of their answers. Replies, grouped by office, are prepared for distribution in leaflet form or sometimes as a special feature for local newspapers. In the questionnaires the League solicits information on the candidate's educational, occupational, and other experience. Questions dealing with policy are usually broadly phrased, and candidates are asked to keep their answers brief. The generality of the questions invites generalities in reply, certainly one

[35] By taking advantage of the new exemption of news interview programs from the equal time provisions of Section 315, networks can now bring major party candidates together on programs with this kind of format, and Robert Sarnoff has indicated that the National Broadcasting Company will ask the 1960 presidential nominees to appear "side by side" on its "Meet the Press Program" in a six program series to begin in September. (*New York Times,* Apr. 22, 1960.) Adlai Stevenson, has recently proposed that the broadcasting media sponsor regular weekly, back-to-back, half-hour programs for major party presidential candidates in the coming election, with a third half hour for rebuttal divided equally between them. ("Plan for a Great Debate," *This Week,* Mar. 6, 1960, p. 14.) If such programs were not to give rise to valid claims for equal time by minor party candidates, however, Section 315 would have to be further revised.

81

of the chief shortcomings of this kind of project. The resulting publication does bring together in one place, however, material that can provide the voter with a basis for at least rudimentary comparisons of candidates and their programs.

Candidate meetings are another characteristic part of the voter service activity of the League. The League invites all candidates for a given office to share the platform in a meeting organized by the League and chaired by a League member. Meetings are scheduled only if all candidates accept. If they agree to appear, they are given an opportunity to make brief pleas in their own behalf. The remainder—and usually the greater part—of the meeting is then devoted to a questioning of the candidates by members of the audience. The technique allows and encourages both cross examination of the candidates and debate between them.[36] In recent years, the League has attempted to bring the benefits of its candidates' meetings to a larger audience through radio and television, and station managers have cooperated by granting public service time. The procedure followed in these broadcasts and telecasts is essentially that of the candidate meeting: a League moderator, joint appearance of candidates, questions from the audience. The most important difference is that the League's inquisitors in these affairs have prepared their questions in advance, and the questioning is, therefore, less spontaneous.

The substantial success the League has had in involving candidates in its programs suggests that the conditions that often lead candidates to avoid questioning and debate are not entirely impervious to conscious efforts to change them. At least two motives incline a candidate toward cooperation with the League, particularly if he is engaged in a close race:

[36] Debate, that is, on policy matters. The League attempts, so far as it is possible, to discourage debate on personal issues in an effort to avoid name calling and personal attacks.

the desire for a forum, on the one hand, and fear, on the other, that refusal to cooperate will antagonize an active and articulate group in the community.

Summary

The argument of this chapter can be brought to a close at this point. Its essential outline has been as follows: Contemporary campaign discussion is often of such a character that it is unlikely to help voters much in their efforts to arrive at a wise choice of public officials. It may, in fact, have quite the reverse effect. Campaign propagandists obscure the real differences between candidates and parties by distortion, by evasiveness, and by talking generalities. That they create new and fictitious ones to replace them can not be regarded as adequate compensation. Many of the forms campaign discussion takes—campaign speeches, spot announcements, advertising, documentaries, "literature," newspaper advertising—both exploit and encourage the fragmentation, passivity, and part-time character of the campaign audience.

Some forms of discussion, however, are much more likely to support rational discourse than others, and this suggests that measures might be taken to increase the contribution of campaign discussion to electoral rationality. Among the measures appropriate to this objective would be: establishing of press conferences as a campaign institution; encouraging interpretative reporting, weekly summaries of campaign news, issue-by-issue feature articles on policy stands taken by candidates, and battle pages; government financing of radio and television debates; revision of Section 315 of the Federal Communications Act to facilitate joint encounters of candidates under the sponsorship of the radio and television networks;

government sponsorship of an altered form of the publicity pamphlet; and organizing forums and debates before private associations and citizens' groups. That such measures would work no magic goes without saying, but they should be considered.

5

Unfair Personal Attacks

A GENERAL ANALYSIS of the discussion of personal issues in campaigns would reveal little that has not already been shown by the analysis of policy discussion. Unfair attacks on candidates merit consideration as a problem distinct from other kinds of shortcomings in campaign discussion, however, for at least two reasons. First of all, the discussion of personality probably has a more consistent importance in political campaigning than does policy controversy. The compromises that accompany the building of majority coalitions, the loose discipline of the two major parties, the holding of elections at fixed intervals, the nomination of candidates in party primaries—all these features of the nation's electoral and party system operate to reduce the impact of policy conflict on elections and to bring personal issues to the front.

Then, too, the discussion of character and personality has a legal dimension that the discussion of other subjects lacks. The wisdom or morality of what campaigners say about public policy may often be disputed, but its legality is rarely open to question. In contrast, the law—specifically the law of defamation—in principle sets limits on what can be said about persons and provides a remedy for victims of defamation in actions for libel and slander.

Unfair personal attacks in campaigns are thus both a legal and a political problem. It is the purpose of the present chapter to consider them in both these perspectives: to examine the forms they take, how they are dealt with by campaigners, and how adequately they are controlled by existing law. It should become clear in the course of this examination that neither the politics of defamation nor the law of defamation can be fruitfully considered without reference to both, and that attempts to control unfair attacks on candidates must take full account of both.

The Politics of Disparagement

As a political phenomenon, unfair personal attacks on candidates are best viewed as the shadow side of campaign emphasis on personality. A politics that makes a well-known name and a favorable public image among the most valuable of political goods, as American politics does, also encourages the disparagement of those who possess these assets. Such disparagement has been, therefore, a frequent, widespread, and ancient feature of political campaigning. "Those who get by without it," Frank Kent has observed, "are either too colorless to make an attack feasible or so sure to be elected as not to make one worthwhile."[1]

Personal attack may take varying forms. Scandalous accusations, spread in anonymous publications or by whispers, have appeared in many campaigns, perhaps in the greater number of those that have been closely fought.[2] In most cases they were in no sense major issues—Kent considers them to have

[1] Frank R. Kent, *Political Behavior* (1928), p. 165. Copyright 1928, Wm. Morrow and Co.

[2] Pendleton Herring lists a number of the more outrageous ones, circulated about Presidents Franklin Roosevelt, Theodore Roosevelt, Grover Cleveland, Ulysses S. Grant, Warren G. Harding, and Thomas Jefferson. See *The Politics of Democracy* (1940), p. 253. See also James Truslow Adams, "Our Whispering Campaigns," *Harper's Magazine* (September 1932), pp. 447-48, Jerome Davis, *Character Assassination* (1950), pp. 18-22 and David Cushman Coyle, *Ordeal of the Presidency* (1960).

86

been primarily the handiwork of local machines designed for an ignorant and gullible audience. On other occasions, however, charges of misconduct have been the central business of the campaign and have been pressed strongly and publicly by responsible, or apparently responsible, persons. They have included accusations of disloyalty, acceptance of bribes, embezzlement, election frauds, and racial prejudice or the lack of it.

What is legitimate or illegitimate in personal attacks is, of course, subject to no absolute definition. There would be few subjects that could not, in certain circumstances, be deemed proper for discussion, although some—the sexual life of a candidate, for example—would generally be considered irrelevant to the choice of office holders and in bad taste. Normally, it would also be considered improper to discuss the shortcomings of persons associated with the candidate by private ties, for example, the alcoholism of a son or daughter.

The substance of charges has less to do with their fairness, however, than does their accuracy and the way in which they are presented. If the discussion of the qualifications of candidates is to contribute to rational electoral decisions, any attack based on falsehood or distortion, or any attack launched at such a time or under such conditions as not to permit reply, must be ruled illegitimate.

In V.O. Key's opinion, "Most smears are lies, nothing more, nothing less."[3] They may be lies that impugn the integrity of a candidate or that simply misrepresent his private or public record. The former kind of charge, for example, was made in a relatively recent primary campaign for the Democratic leadership of New York County's 8th Assembly District North, where the incumbent leader and his followers distributed a campaign newspaper that termed his opponent a "fellow traveler" and "a notorious champion of communists

[3] *Politics, Parties and Pressure Groups* (1958), p. 20.

and seditionists."[4] An instance of the latter occurred in a Mississippi primary campaign where a local publisher used his editorial columns to criticize a state representative's vote for a bill redesignating certain state highways. The editorial contained a number of false statements that gave an erroneous view of what the legislator had done and, according to testimony, aroused a good deal of sentiment against him. The statement did not, however, reflect on his honesty or integrity. It was politically damaging, but not damaging to reputation.[5]

A clever propagandist, in the discussion of candidates as in the discussion of any other subject, can also do much to mislead the public without making statements that are demonstrably false. He may, for example, exaggerate the importance or distort the meaning of a candidate's incidental personal associations and organizational affiliations. John T. Flynn has described the technique as follows:

> First it is necessary to select what I call a Smear Carrier. Some person who is either guilty or actually convicted of an offense is selected. He is loaded with infamy for all to see. He, however, is not the real intended victim. The real victim is some prominent Senator or Congressman or political or business leader or writer against whom nothing could be proved and who could not be libeled with impunity. Having completely covered the Smear Carrier with guilt, the smearer proceeds to link him with the real victim. He merely mentions that the intended victim knows the Smear Carrier, or that he has written him a letter or got one from him or received him in his office or appeared at some public meeting with him.[6]

If their names are associated frequently enough, Flynn observes, it will not be long before the intended victim "is as effectively smeared as the Smear Carrier whose guilt has been

[4] See *Toomey* v. *Farley*, 138 N.E. 2d 221 (1956), and *New York Times*, Oct. 20, 1956.

[5] For a more extensive account of the case, see *Manasco* v. *Walley*, 216 Mississippi 614 (1942).

[6] John T. Flynn, *The Smear Terror* (1947), pp. 3-4.

'splashed' on him.''[7] Again, however, distortion need not cast reflection on a candidate's integrity to be damaging; it may simply falsify his record. Thus, in the 1950 Ohio senatorial campaign an opposition pamphlet implied that the late Senator Robert A. Taft opposed any increase in the minimum wage rate by charging that he had opposed a bill that would have raised the minimum wage rate to sixty-five cents. This charge—aimed at a labor audience—was technically true but completely misleading, since Taft had opposed the measure only because he was supporting an alternative one that would have put the minimum wage at seventy-five cents.

The timing of attacks is also a frequent source of their unfairness. This is true when they occur so near the end of a campaign that an effective answer is all but impossible. Such a tactic was used against former Senator Millard Tydings in his unsuccessful campaign for re-election in 1950. Four days before election day, his opponents distributed a four page tabloid violently attacking the Senator for his role in an investigation of Communist influence in the Department of State. The tabloid contained, among other items, a composite picture intended to convey the false impression that Tydings had engaged in a friendly conversation with the Communist leader, Earl Browder.

There are few politicians who are not in some degree vulnerable to such tactics. Accusations of misconduct in office have a certain prima facie credibility to voters both because there have been numerous instances of such misconduct and because the public is prone to attribute certain kinds of sins to politicians as a class.[8] Moreover, a man who has followed a po-

---

[7] *Ibid.*

[8] In a study of public attitudes toward politicians, the National Opinion Research Center found that many people consider politics and corruption to be natural companions. Forty-eight per cent of the respondents believed it almost impossible for a man to stay honest in politics. National Opinion Research Center, *The Public Looks At Politics and Politicians*, Report No. 20 (March 1944).

litical career is almost certain to have been in contact with persons of dubious character or to have been in situations susceptible of misrepresentation.[9] This being true, it is easy, as Bryce remarked, "to gather up rumors, piece out old though unproved stories of corruption, put the worst meaning on doubtful words, and so construct a damning impeachment."[10]

The impeachment does not need to command the positive belief of any considerable number of voters to be damaging to its victim and subversive of the educational function of campaigning. The purposes of those who have launched the attack may be well enough served if it merely raises doubt about a candidate's fitness for office—tarnishes, not blackens him—or if it diverts discussion from some issue they wish to avoid. False charges may, for example, be used to counter a legitimate attack with the result that—again in Bryce's words —"the plain citizen, hearing much which he cannot believe, finding foul imputations brought even against those he has reason to respect, despairs of sifting the evidence in any given case, and sets down most of the charges to malice and 'campaign methods,' while concluding that the residue is about equally true of all politicians alike."[11]

The plain citizen is likely to despair of sifting evidence in particular cases for at least two reasons. When a candidate has been charged with corrupt dealings or improper associations, much of the evidence required for judgment on the issue will not be a matter of public record—certainly not in the same

[9] Thus Walter Quigley, a Minnesota public relations man who has made a profession of preparing attacks on candidates, writes that "I certainly like to campaign against a man who has written a book or has several hundred votes in Congress or a legislature. No matter how sincere he may be, one can take a couple of dozen of these votes or paragraphs from the book and crucify him." Quoted from a letter in Frank H. Jonas, "The Art of Political Dynamiting," *The Western Political Quarterly* (June 1957), p. 378n.
[10] James Bryce, *The American Commonwealth* (1890), Vol. 2, p. 210.
[11] *Ibid.*

sense that the policy actions of government are. Furthermore, campaigners often fail to bring the available evidence into campaign discussion, because it is not in their short-run interest to do so. When attacked, they are less likely to give their side of the story than they are either to ignore the charges completely or to counterattack.

Frank Kent has described a case that, in his opinion, was "one of the best examples of effective ignoring of an opponent that has ever occurred in politics."[12] The hero of his story is the late Senator Arthur P. Gorman of Maryland, strongly challenged in a re-election campaign by Isidor Rayner, later a senator, and by the *Baltimore Sun*. Rayner, in the middle of the campaign, wrote Gorman a letter, in which he accused the organization of a series of specific crimes and challenged him to a public debate. The letter was sent to Gorman special delivery and was printed in full in the *Sun*. When reporters asked Gorman what his reply was to be, the Senator feigned ignorance of the affair, said he had had no chance to look at his mail, and had missed reading the *Sun*. He continued the pose for four days, until "the State got to laughing. The *Sun* and Rayner had been so tense and excited about the challenge, they had played it up so dramatically, that the calmness with which Gorman ignored it could not fail to make both the paper and the politician ridiculous. They were both glad to drop it before the end of the week."[13] Kent, who has attempted to sum up practical political wisdom on the politics of personal attack, advised that a candidate is wise to follow Gorman's example whenever a charge or accusation seems unlikely to affect the outcome of the election.

Attacks aimed directly at a candidate's fitness for office, if pressed insistently, will normally evoke some more positive response than that just noted. One such reaction, again de-

[12] Frank Kent, *op. cit.*, p. 168.
[13] *Ibid.*, p. 171.

scribed by Kent, "is to set up the cry of 'mud slinging.' "[14]
The rule, Kent observes, is to charge your opponent with trying to destroy your reputation and "to bring in your wife and
children, to say that you do not mind this effort to wreck your
good name yourself; you can stand it but they cannot."[15] In
the 1952 campaign both parts of this rule were followed almost literally by Vice-President, then Senator, Richard Nixon
in his now famous reply to charges that he had improperly
accepted money from some of his supporters. At one point he
charged that "The purpose of the smear, I know, is this, to
silence me, to make me let up."[16] At another, he said that he
hoped the politicians would not criticize him for another gift
he had accepted, the celebrated dog Checkers, because "the
kids, like all kids, loved the dog."[17]

Another frequent response to personal attack is to reply
with countercharges. In essence, this was the strategy adopted
by the late Robert A. Taft in his 1950 campaign for the Senate. Although Taft prepared detailed answers to charges
brought against him, he sent such material to two specialized
audiences—newspaper editors and his own campaign workers.[18] For the general public, he adopted another tactic: "The
other course I pursued," he told senators investigating the
campaign, "was to unmask the source of this propaganda [that
used against him]. We publicized the fact that the CIO Political Action Committee had prepared the Black Book, which
was the basis of all these charges, and I undertook to describe

[14] *Ibid.*, p. 172.
[15] *Ibid.*, p. 173.
[16] *U. S. News and World Report* (Oct. 3, 1952).
[17] *Ibid.*
[18] See *Investigation into the 1950 Ohio Senatorial Campaign,* Hearings before the Senate Committee on Rules and Administration, 82 Cong. 1 and
2 sess., p. 51. Senator Taft's statement was: "These were long statements and
I only sent them to the editors, and to Taft chairmen in each county. I wanted
my chairmen to know the answers and be able to enter denials, if any particular lie seemed to be making headway with the people of their district."

to the people of Ohio the character of the CIO Political Action Committee."[19] In one phase of his counter-attack, Taft charged that the entire campaign against him had been "blue-printed" by the convicted Communist, Gus Hall.

From the campaigner's point of view, strategies of the kind just reviewed are normally sounder ways of dealing with personal attacks than any kind of point-by-point defense would be. This is true for several reasons: First, an answer to accusations may be difficult to put into a simple and convincing message that can be conveyed adequately to a mass electorate in a short length of time. Second, the campaigner can rarely be sure that answers will reach the same audiences that have heard the accusations, and a politician may do himself more harm than good by giving them further publicity. Third, a candidate usually cannot answer charges once and for all, since the attacking side is most probably prepared to issue them in a new form. A candidate who begins to defend himself is, therefore, in serious danger of fighting the remainder of the campaign on ground chosen by the opposition.

Thus the discussion of personal issues in campaigns often has little to do with presenting evidence on the truth or falsity of particular charges. This fact, as has already been noted, makes it difficult for the electorate to decide such issues on their merits. It also means that public opinion must play a less effective role in deterring unfair attacks than that which theorists have often assigned to it. The politician's tactics in responding to personal attack may be useful in minimizing its damage to him at the polls, but they do not yield the kind of information voters need if they are to decide whether the attack was fair or unfair.

[19] *Ibid.,* p. 52.

The Law of Defamation

The picture just drawn of the politics of personal attack is modified, but not altered substantially, by the fact that candidates can bring actions for libel and slander against their accusers. The possibility of a libel suit almost certainly makes those who plan to question a candidate's integrity choose their words more cautiously than would otherwise be the case. For example, a public relations man, commenting on the work of a co-professional, observes that the latter "knows the value of absolute accuracy in the material he uses. Never, to my knowledge, has he been caught in the meshes of libel or successfully challenged. He can be utterly ruthless and make the most respected individual appear to be a downright scalawag, but there is never anything upon which a libel pleading can be based."[20] The law of defamation has too limited an application to campaign propaganda, however, to make it in any sense an answer to the problems being discussed here.

This is true partly because of the way defamation has been defined. In law, defamatory communications are those that injure personal reputation.[21] Thus, the class of statements for which a man may hope to win a suit for libel or slander by no means includes all those that can reasonably be termed unfair or all those that impair the value of the campaign discussion of personal issues. For a great many true but misleading statements and for many false statements that injure a candidate politically but do not injure his reputation, there is no legal remedy in an action for defamation.

[20] See Frank H. Jonas, *op. cit.*, p. 388.

[21] A standard authority defines the offense as follows: "A communication is defamatory if it tends so to harm the reputation of another as to lower him in the estimation of the community or to deter third persons from associating or dealing with him." 3 Restatement of Torts, sec. 559.

94

Candidates and public officials, moreover, receive less protection even against clearly defamatory publications than do most of their fellow citizens. Under the rule of fair comment, as it is interpreted in a majority of the states, a candidate has an actionable case only when he can show that attacks on him were malicious or contained false statements of fact. This is as far as courts are now willing to go in restricting campaign defamation. Comments or opinions on facts truly stated, provided they express the critics real views, are not actionable. Such comments need not be either fair or reasonable inferences from fact, and in this respect the doctrine of fair comment is misleadingly named.[22]

In a sizable number of states, alternative rules are applied that further lessen a candidate's chances to collect for injuries to reputation. In order of the severity with which they restrict discussion, these are the New Hampshire rule, the so-called minority rule, the doctrine of libel per se, and the public official rule. In New Hampshire, a defendant escapes liability for false and defamatory statements of fact if he can show that he had reasonable grounds for believing them true. Under the minority rule, a candidate-plaintiff must establish not only that the defendant made false statements, but that he did so knowingly. The doctrine of libel per se requires that a defamed candidate show that pecuniary loss resulted from the libel, except in cases where he has been charged with a crime or some other gross delinquency. Under the public official

[22] The reason for this legal distinction between fact and comment has been explained as follows: "To state accurately what a man has done, and then to say that in your opinion such conduct is disgraceful or dishonorable, is comment which may do no harm, as everyone can judge for himself whether the opinion expressed is well founded or not. Misdescription of conduct, on the other hand, only leads to one conclusion detrimental to the person whose conduct is misdescribed and leaves the reader no opportunity for judging for himself the character of the conduct condemned, nothing but a false picture being presented for judgment." *Christie* v. *Robertson,* 10 New South Wales L.R. 157, quoted in Van Vechten Veeder, "Freedom of Public Discussion," *Harvard Law Review* (April 1910), pp. 423-24.

rule, a charge to be actionable "must be of such a nature that if true it would be cause for . . . removal from office."[23]

The import of all these rules can be put in a few words. In any action for defamation the defamed candidate cannot hope to win a favorable verdict unless he can show that statements of fact made in charges against him are untrue. And in some jurisdictions he can lose his case even after demonstrating that such charges are false.

If this fact makes it safe for campaigners to denounce their opponents with considerable freedom in campaign speeches and literature, two other rules applied in defamation cases sometimes allow them to use materials in which denunciation can be equally, or still more, unrestrained. The first of these bars any legal recourse in an action for defamation for anything said or written by members of Congress or of state legislatures in the exercise of legislative duties, even though what has been said is clearly defamatory, completely false, and maliciously published. The same rule applies in the case of statements made by witnesses appearing before legislative committees; by the parties, counsel, judge, or jury in a judicial proceeding; and by certain executive officers in the course of conducting official business. Statements made on all these occasions enjoy an *absolute privilege*. The second rule precludes a libel or slander action against anyone who gives voters a fair and accurate report of anything said on an occasion of absolute privilege—though both false and defamatory—unless it can be proved that he did so from malice. Such a report enjoys a *conditional* or *qualified* privilege. An example, perhaps, will make more evident what these two rules can mean for campaigning.

On July 16, 1940, a subcommittee of the Un-American Ac-

[23] The words of a Texas court applying this rule. See Dix W. Noel, "Defamation of Public Officers and Candidates," *Columbia Law Review* (November 1949), pp. 875-903, for a discussion of both libel *per se* and the public official rule.

tivities Committee took testimony in an executive session at Beaumont, Texas. The committee's chairman, Martin Dies, was the only member of Congress in attendance. This subcommittee of one heard a witness, John L. Leech, testify that he had seen Representative Franck R. Havenner of San Francisco in attendance at a meeting of the California Communist Party Executive Committee. The hearing went on as follows:

> Question. Could he [Havenner] have attended this meeting if he had not been a member of the Communist Party?
>
> Answer. No; I have never known of a case, and I don't believe such a connection has ever taken place where a nonmember could meet with a leading body of the party.[24]

Leech further reported that he had met with Havenner on other occasions "informally, in left-wing affairs" and that Havenner had "participated in affairs organized by the Communist party or left-wing organizations under the domination of the Communist party."[25] This testimony, presumably, was absolutely privileged.

The House of Representatives heard Havenner's side of the story some five years later. In a speech from the floor, he denied categorically that he had ever been a member or had any association with the Communist party; that he had any sympathy with the Communist party, its platforms, or principles; that he knew Leech; or that he had ever attended a Communist party meeting. Many of his colleagues, Democrats and Republicans, took the occasion to assure Havenner that they thought his loyalty beyond question. In comments on Havenner's speech, Representatives Jerry Voorhis and Noah M. Mason, both of whom had been members of the Un-American Activities Committee at the time of the Beaumont hearings, stated that they had been completely unaware that the committee's records contained any such charges.

[24] *Congressional Record*, Vol. 91, Pt. 1, 79 Cong. 1 sess., p. 206.
[25] *Ibid.*

Havenner himself had learned of Leech's testimony, not from Chairman Dies, but from his opponents in the previous year's campaign. On October 30, 1944, a few days before the end of that campaign, the San Francisco *Chronicle* carried an advertisement headed, "WOULD YOU TRUST YOUR POST-WAR FUTURE IN THESE HANDS?" The body of the advertisement was a verbatim reproduction of a portion of the Leech testimony, substantially as it has been quoted above. Had Havenner gone to court, this material, though not absolutely privileged, presumably would have been held conditionally privileged as a fair and accurate account of a legislative proceeding. If so, he would have been without remedy unless he could have proved malice, something that it is never easy to do.

It should be evident from this example that the two privileges are open to serious abuse. With the cooperation of a friendly congressman, libelous materials may be introduced into legislative records, reports, and hearings. If used later in a campaign, they can rarely be challenged successfully in a libel action.

A suit for libel is not the only remedy that exists for offenses of this kind, but, as the Havenner case demonstrates, the alternatives to it often do not operate, or operate only with great delay. Congressman Havenner was not informed of the charges against him. He was given no chance to testify on his own behalf. No further investigation of the charges was made, although he requested such an investigation. No disciplinary action was taken against Chairman Dies. No action for perjury was brought against Leech. The charges were finally expunged from the records of the Committee on Un-American Activities on June 15, 1948—but that was seven years, eleven months after the event.

Despite the obviously restricted application of the law of defamation to political campaigning that is shown by this review of its relevant rules, legal scholars seem to be generally agreed that there are many more legally actionable cases of defamation involving candidates than are ever brought to court.[26] At first glance, this failure of candidates to seek an available remedy is surprising. It is not so if one considers the matter from the politician's point of view: politically, a successful libel or slander suit may either be of little value to a candidate or may actually do him harm.

In cases of defamation, the legal process is out of phase with the political process. At the time of an attack, a candidate can do little more than register a protest by filing suit. He may have a very long time to wait before the court hands down a verdict. The reaction of a former candidate for the United States Senate to this fact is probably typical: "It is little consolation to the candidate and none to the voters to have the persons guilty of an unfair attack respond in damages months or years after the election."[27] If the verdict is favorable, a candidate-plaintiff's gain is more financial than political, given the traditional silence of much of the press regarding libel actions. While charges against a candidate are likely to have been given full publicity, his vindication in court will probably receive scant attention. Under these conditions, a successful action for defamation can do little to help the candidate as a candidate and politician.

When a candidate files suit for libel, moreover, he does so at the risk of further injury to his reputation. "In actions for defamation," writes Martin Newell, "it is well settled that the plaintiff's general character is involved in the issue; and evidence showing what it is, and consequently its true value, may

---

[26] See Noel, *op. cit.*, p. 875; David Riesman, "Democracy and Defamation: Fair Game and Fair Comment II," *Columbia Law Review* (November 1942), p. 1284; Morris L. Ernst and Alexander Lindey, *Hold Your Tongue!* (1950), p. 57; Richard C. Donnelly, "The Right of Reply: An Alternative to an action for Libel," *Virginia Law Review* (November 1948), p. 884.

[27] From a letter to the author.

be offered upon either side to affect the amount of damages."[28]
In about half the states, this kind of evidence is confined to
the particular trait attacked. In some, however, defendants
are allowed to present evidence of the plaintiff's bad character, and, as a general practice, the plaintiff can be questioned
at length about particular instances of misconduct if he takes
the stand on his own behalf.[29] An action for libel may thus
provide a forum for new charges and defamatory insinuations,
on an occasion that is privileged. "Often," observes Riesman,
"the more reputable the plaintiff, the more likely he is to be
deterred by the prospect of buried misdeeds being brought
out in his cross-examination."[30]

An array of popular attitudes, finally, may turn a legally
sound case into a politically uncertain one. There is some
tendency on the part of voters to feel that politicians should
be "scrappers," that they should be able to "take it," that they
should let bygones be bygones, that they should not be "hard
losers." A Texas public relations man writes, for example,
"the candidate does not need any new laws to protect him. If
he is thin-skinned he should get out of politics."[31] A Delaware
party official, commenting on the precautions taken by present day newspapers in avoiding libel suits, observes: "I am
frank to say that I find the more colorful accounts of former
years far more interesting than those of today."[32] No one
knows how widespread or deep-seated such attitudes are, but
politicians are convinced enough of their reality to fear them.

---

[28] Martin L. Newell, *The Law of Slander and Libel* (1914), 3rd ed., p. 1053.
[29] Richard C. Donnelly, "The Law of Defamation: Proposals for Reform,"
Minnesota Law Review (May 1949), pp. 619-20.
[30] Riesman, *op. cit.*, p. 1285.
[31] In a letter to the author.
[32] In a letter to the author.

Problems of Control

From what has been said, it should be clear that a search for new methods to control unfair personal attacks on candidates is in order. Such attacks impair the value of campaign discussion by their tendency to mislead voters, to smother discussion of genuine issues of policy and personality, and to foster indiscriminate suspicion of all campaign talk. They can also, as one student of public administration has observed, be held partly responsible for the low prestige of politics as a profession and for the government's difficulty in recruiting able men for the elective public service.[33] Neither existing law nor current political practice adequately protect the public interest in this area.

Proposals to strengthen legal controls, however, raise one basic question of public policy: At what point should the balance be struck between the public's interest in free discussion and its interest in the integrity of elections? Although the courts of a majority of the states hold critics of candidates accountable for false statements of fact, some legal scholars and a minority of the states have been unwilling to go so far. The two positions are in direct contradiction: Those who hold the minority view, most authoritatively stated in *Cole-*

---

[33] George A. Graham, *Morality in American Politics* (1952), p. 281. In Woodrow Wilson's opinion, expressed in a letter written in 1912, "Misrepresentation is the penalty which men in public life must expect in the course of their effort to render service. The unfortunate fact is that there are probably hundreds of men in America of first rate intellectual force, of genuine public spirit and broad patriotism, who would be of immeasurable value to public service, but who are deterred from entering it because they shrink from this particular penalty. They prefer to pursue private careers, rather than expose themselves and their families to unfounded criticism and attack, and the country is thereby impoverished." Quoted in Arthur S. Link, *Wilson: The Road to the White House* (1947), pp. 389-90.

man v. *MacLennan*, do not deny the harm done by false and unfounded accusations but argue that "the importance to the state and to society of such discussions is so vast and the advantages derived are so great that they more than counterbalance the inconvenience of private persons whose conduct may be involved, and occasional injury to the reputations of individuals must yield to the public welfare, although at times such injury may be great."[34] Proponents of the majority rule argue in rebuttal that "the danger that honorable and worthy men may be driven from politics and public service by allowing too great latitude in attacks upon their characters outweighs any benefit that might occasionally accrue to the public from charges of corruption that are true in fact but are incapable of legal proof."[35]

Which of these views ought to guide the search for new legal remedies? Obviously, the relative weight of the losses and gains that attend adoption of either rule cannot be nicely calculated. On the whole, however, the majority rule seems to reflect a better appreciation of all the interests at stake and a more realistic view of the political factors involved.

It is not fair to phrase the issue as one of injury to private reputation *versus* full information to the electorate, as does the opinion in *Coleman* v. *MacLennan*. Though damage to reputation is undoubtedly one consequence of unfair personal attacks, it is certainly not their only consequence and probably not the most important one. False charges do as much, or more, injury to the public's interest in accurate information about the qualifications of candidates and to its interest in maintaining the prestige of the public service. A more accurate statement of the issue would be this: Do the advantages to be gained by encouraging critics to air suspicions for which

[34] *Coleman* v. *MacLennan*, 78 Kansas 711 (1908).
[35] The words of William Howard Taft, then a judge of the 6th Circuit, in *Post Publishing Company* v. *Hallam*, 59 Fed. 530 (1893).

they have no legal proof outweigh the injuries such a policy would work on all these interests? Obviously, there would be some loss if men hesitated to bring official misconduct to public attention until they had evidence that would convince a court of law. Making a charge, as David Riesman has argued, may be the only way to prove it. Such action can sometimes "force an investigation, rally others to come forward with bits of proof in their possession or maneuver [the accused person] himself into damaging admissions."[36]

While this is a valid observation, it must be remembered that the majority rule is not really so restrictive as Riesman's argument implies. It does not prevent critics from commenting on questionable conduct. Neither does it absolutely prevent them from hurling charges for which they lack proof; it simply holds them accountable if such charges cannot be proved. If a man accuses another of misconduct, making it possible for people "to come forward with bits of proof in their possession" or to extract damaging admission from the accused, he would not seem to be unduly penalized if required to make amends in the event that he was mistaken.

Moreover, a court is in several ways better equipped to determine the truth or falsity of accusations than is the public as a whole. One might even say that courts are designed to settle such questions—they are constantly in the business of determining the accuracy of allegations that particular individuals have conducted themselves in particular ways. A court of law, unlike the so-called court of public opinion, is in a position to compel witnesses, hear evidence on their credibility, and hold them responsible for perjury. Its procedures do much to ensure that the evidence on both sides of an issue will be fully presented. It is to the advantage of the public, therefore, to have factual questions of personal misconduct referred to the courts, assuming a nonpartisan judiciary. The

[36] Riesman, *op. cit.*, p. 1291*n*.

courts can, in effect, act as a fact-finding agency for the electorate.

If they are to play such a role, however, solutions must be found to two difficult problems. One of these is how to increase the effect of court action on the conduct of campaign discussion. At present, the law of defamation can be effective only as a deterrent. Courts do not reach a verdict on cases of defamation swiftly enough to allow voters to take that decision into account when they render their own. Moreover, the law as it now stands serves at most to deter factual inaccuracies in statements derogatory to reputation. It offers no remedies for nondefamatory falsehoods or for unfair practices that do not involve falsehood.

How to bring cases involving candidates into courts is a second problem. At present, there are two methods for enforcing the law of defamation: A civil suit for damages and criminal prosecution. The shortcomings of the former as a way to secure court action in political cases have already been discussed. The defects of the latter seem, if anything, to be even greater. Criminal prosecutions must be initiated by public prosecutors. These, in many instances, are elected officials who may do their own political careers considerable damage if they take such a responsibility too seriously. In any event, it would appear ill-advised to depend on partisan officials for an even-handed and consistent prosecution of offenses that are so directly tied to partisan conflict.

Summary

From the foregoing analysis of personal attacks on candidates, we should be prepared to reach the following conclusions. The character of the choice that faces voters in American elections—one between men and not between unified parties committed to definite policy programs—gives campaigners exceedingly strong motives to attack the personal qualifications of opposition candidates. When they have not been able to do so fairly, they have often done so unfairly, making unfair personal attacks a persistent feature of our campaigns. Their persistence and frequency merit concern. Whether or not such attacks mean the loss of an election to their victim, the community as a whole loses, for the community has an interest in protecting private reputation, preserving respect for elective public office, and in not being diverted from the consideration of real issues to the consideration of false ones. At the present time we rely almost entirely on voters and on courts of law to discourage unfair attacks. Neither is really in a position to do so effectively. The strategies candidates find it expedient to adopt in responding to their attackers normally do not include the presentation of the evidence that voters would need to judge the fairness or unfairness of accusations nor do they normally involve appeals to the courts. The protection offered candidates by the law of defamation is more apparent than real because it is, in the final analysis, so meager, and because it fails to take account of the political motives of defamed candidates. The problems involved in finding more effective ways of discouraging unfair attacks are not beyond remedy, but that is the subject of the next chapter.

6

Curbing Unfair Personal Attacks

THE PRECEDING CHAPTER stated the two principal problems involved in developing effective legal controls for unfair attacks on candidates; the present one will outline some possible solutions to those problems. Before doing so, however, some nonlegal measures to combat abuses need to be considered, for their control is not simply a problem for legislators. Law alone is not an adequate instrument for dealing with malpractices in campaigns, and legal controls, even technically well-designed ones, can hardly be fully effective without some kind of support in public opinion.

Both the press and citizen groups, therefore, have a role to play in this area. The press, in reporting campaigns, can shape the discussion of personal issues just as it can shape policy discussion. Citizen groups can call public attention to the consequences of unfair tactics, can define standards of good conduct, and can aid in law enforcement.

Action by Press and Public

Since the kinds of abuses that occur in the discussion of personal issues differ little from those in policy discussion, the press can help to put such issues in a form that contributes to rational electoral decisions in much the same way. It can strive to give reasonably full and equal coverage to accusations and responses to accusations. It can attempt to give accusations and responses equally favorable display and, insofar as possible, to publish them in the same story or in adjoining stories. Periodically, it can give summaries of the evidence presented on both sides.

The press is in a particularly good position to combat one kind of unfair practice—the last minute attack. In fact, press action is perhaps the most promising way of dealing with this kind of abuse. The advice of J. Russell Wiggins, Executive Editor of the *Washington Post and Times Herald*, on this subject is worth quoting in full:

> In the closing days of a campaign, we must be especially careful that we do not help float groundless accusations and libelous rumors to which the persons accused cannot answer before the election. The news columns are the proper forum for debate, but debate there, as elsewhere, must be conducted with regard for the rules of fairness. Election day editions ought to be confined to the real news of the election and should shun speeches and statements making last minute charges, the truth or falsity of which cannot be ascertained, or the answers to which cannot be simultaneously presented.[1]

Were campaigners to know that the last minute attack would normally be met by press silence, the incentive for using such tactics would be considerably reduced.

Reporting personal issues in this way means, of course, that the press must see its responsibility as requiring more of it than mere service as a common carrier for charges and counter charges whenever they occur, at whomever they are directed, and in whatever language they are expressed. It means also that the press has not discharged all its obligations to the public when its reports do not offend the letter of the law of

[1] Memorandum to staff, March 15, 1956.

libel. As Mr. Wiggins puts this sterner conception of press responsibility:

> Whatever the law in the matter, we do not wish to work injustice on individual persons during a campaign or at any other time. When someone is charged with criminal acts, great care must be taken in reporting. If we are satisfied the matter is not libelous or is privileged . . . we should take care to see that accusation and answer are printed in the same editions of the newspaper, if possible.[2]

If it is not possible to print accusations and replies together, it would seem good practice for editors to include in their original reports of charges all information useful in assessing their accuracy.

The activities of two committees give an indication of the potential role that citizen groups might play in the control of unfair attacks on candidates. One of these is Philadelphia's Committee of Seventy, a nonpartisan group that carries on an educational program for improvements in municipal government, criticizes the conduct of government, and helps to police elections. The other is the Fair Campaign Practices Committee (F.C.P.C.), likewise a nonpartisan organization, whose stated purpose is "raising ethical standards in political campaigns." The Committee of Seventy was founded in 1904 as a municipal reform group in what was then a machine-ridden city. The F.C.P.C. was formed in 1954 after "a rash of fast and loose accusations of 'softness' or lack of due diligence toward communism . . . helped to divert attention from records and issues" in the campaigns of the early fifties.[3] The concerns of the two committees, and their approaches to the problems of campaigns and elections, reflect the concerns, values, and approaches to political action of the times that brought them into being: The Committee of Seventy has mainly worked to

[2] *Ibid.*

[3] Charles P. Taft, "Campaign to Stop the Campaign Smear," *New York Times Magazine* (Oct. 12, 1958), p. 82.

prevent election frauds. The F.C.P.C. has given most of its attention to the problem posed by smear tactics, and the greater part of its activity has been directed toward increasing public awareness of that problem.

The two most important projects of the F.C.P.C. to date have been the preparation of post-election reports on smears and the pre-election solicitation of public declarations by candidates that they will adhere to the principles of the committee's "Code of Fair Campaign Practices" in the conduct of their campaigns. In its survey of electioneering in 1956 the committee found, according to its chairman, that the facts "did not square at all with the initial report about the ethical level of the '56 campaign. In twenty-six states one or both parties claimed one or more their candidates had been smeared."[4] One senator had had the alleged facts of his love life exposed in a campaign brochure. Another candidate was attacked in a piece of campaign literature that featured photographic reproductions of an old newspaper clipping reporting his indictment on an embezzlement charge but made no mention of his later exoneration. In other instances, a teetotaling candidate was attacked as a drunkard, and a candidate who drank moderately was described as a prohibitionist intent on restricting the sale of liquor in the resort areas of his state. The committee released such findings to the press, included them in materials circulated to schools and civic groups, and used them as the basis for the popular magazine article by Mr. Taft that has been cited above.

In its second major project, the collection of pledges by candidates to abide by its Code of Fair Campaign Practices, the committee has had great success. In 1956 the pledge was signed by one or both candidates in 75 per cent of contested congressional districts, and by both candidates in 102 of the 356 contests. In 1958 one or both candidates in 85 per cent of

4 *Ibid.*

all congressional, senatorial, and gubernatorial contests signed. The committee is under no illusion that its code is self-enforcing—the campaign for signatures is mainly a device to publicize the problem of smears. During the campaign it releases periodic counts on the number of signatures that it has obtained and is rewarded for its efforts both by news coverage of its activities and editorial comment on its aims.[5]

A long run, and more ambitious, objective of the F.C.P.C. is that of winning public acceptance of, and support for, its conception of fair campaigning. Its code, based on the 1951 report of the Subcommittee on Privileges and Elections of the Senate Rules Committee, condemns the use in campaigns of personal vilification, character defamation, whispering campaigns, libel, slander, scurrilous attacks on any candidate or his personal or family life, appeals to racial and religious prejudice, and any material that "misrepresents, distorts, or otherwise falsifies the facts regarding any candidate, as well as the use of malicious or unfounded accusations against any candidate which aim at creating or exploiting doubts, without justification, as to his loyalty or patriotism."[6] Candidates who do not repudiate the support of groups or individuals who use such tactics are regarded as themselves guilty of unfair campaign practices.

There is little in such a code, of course, that anyone could regard as more than a demand that candidates behave in con-

[5] In 1956 Chairman Paul Butler of the Democratic National Committee used the occasion of a joint signing of the pledge with Republican Chairman Leonard Hall to remark: "Fraudulent and baseless charges like 'party of treason' and 'traitorous conduct' not only violate the code, but endanger our whole political system." This prompted Hall to reply, "That's a pretty strange start when you sign a pledge for a fair campaign." Though the incident led at least one newspaper to report it under a headline reading, "Party War So Calmed You Hear Truce Snap," the committee regarded the publicity that attended it as a net gain. See *Washington Post and Times Herald*, May 18, 1956.

[6] Quoted from the Code of Fair Campaign Practices.

formity with standards of conduct generally regarded as right. The F.C.P.C. is aware of this, as well as of the fact that verbal allegiance to its principles does not necessarily mean real acceptance of them either by the political community or the community at large. It regards the formal statement of these principles as only one way in which the committee hopes to combat tacit allegiance to a far less stringent conception of acceptable campaign behavior. A program carried on in schools and civic groups to acquaint people with the code, to show the consequences of failures to realize it, and to show how breaches of it can be recognized is another.

This latter aspect of the committee's work—that of showing voters how to identify smears in concrete cases—is certainly one of the most important contributions that a citizen group could make to discouraging the use of such tactics. Worthy as it is, however, this objective is only partially attainable. The F.C.P.C. has been able to do little more than to identify a few practices that may reasonably be regarded as unfair and prima facie evidence that a candidate is carrying on a smear campaign—clipped and composite photographs, anonymous literature, whispering campaigns, undocumented assertions, and last minute attacks. To do more than this would require the committee to pass judgment on the substantive issues involved in personal attacks, and, unfortunately, no simple formula exists for distinguishing smears from legitimate attacks on these grounds. Smears do not come labeled as such. Instead, they often appear as plausible accusations which, if true, would make the accused unfit for public office.

Wisely, if one thinks of the difficulties it would have encountered, the F.C.P.C. has declined to involve itself in deciding the merits of particular disputes, although it was pressed to do so in the 1958 California gubernatorial campaign by both Chairman Butler of the Democratic National Committee and by Joseph P. Kamp. The latter's pamphlet, attacking Walter Reuther as a "vile purveyor of vicious slander" and a "ruthless, reckless, lawless labor goon" had been distributed by Senator William Knowland's campaign headquarters. Butler asked the F.C.P.C. to censure the use of the pamphlet, and Kamp offered to stop its circulation if the F.C.P.C., after a hearing, decided that the charges leveled against Kamp by the Democrats were justified. Chairman Taft declined to grant Kamp's request. If the committee had done otherwise, it would have arrogated to itself the function of a court, but without a court's ability to gather evidence and compel witnesses.

A private group, once it has made voters aware of the problems caused by smearing, has won genuine acceptance for a code of fair conduct, and has shown the unfairness involved in certain kinds of tactics, reaches the limits of action by non-legal means. All these things are obviously essential if unfair attacks on candidates are to be brought under control, but it is also clear that doing them is not enough to realize that objective. This suggests a further contribution citizen groups might make to promoting the integrity of elections. They could work for the enforcement of laws designed to curb smears.

Calling violations of the election laws to the attention of enforcement authorities has been an important part of the Committee of Seventy's civic action program. Over the years, the committee has filed complaints in hundreds of cases involving political activity by merit system civil servants, illegal assistance to voters, ballot box stuffing, multiple voting, violation of the secrecy of the ballot, fraudulent returns, and fraudulent registration. In the first six years of its operation, the committee obtained convictions in 250 cases involving offenses of this kind, and in the period 1905-1937 it was responsible for the removal from the voting lists of the names of over 500,000 unqualified voters.[7]

A similar role for groups interested primarily in curbing unfair attacks on candidates must wait on the enactment of laws adequate to that purpose. In this respect, at least, effective action against smears by citizens groups is tied to the problem of securing effective laws against smears.

Substantive Revisions in Law

At this point it will be useful to restate the two main problems involved in the legal control of unfair attacks on candidates. They are: (1) how to make legally actionable certain tactics that impair the value of the discussion of personal issues in campaigns but that are not prohibited by law; and (2) how to bring cases involving such offenses to court; that is, how to secure the enforcement of laws in this field. These problems can be treated separately, both because they are analytically separable and because there is at present no one law or body of law bearing on the problem of smears that offers a model for future legislation. Some states have enacted statutes that give candidates protection against a wide range of offenses but have provided no effective enforcement procedure for them. Others have better enforcement procedures but give candidates little substantive protection.

If the courts are to play a more effective role in curbing unfair attacks on candidates, at least four modifications in the substantive provisions of federal and state election laws should be seriously considered. They are: (1) making politically injurious false statements actionable, as well as false statements

---

[7] "The Committee of Seventy, What Makes it Tick" (typescript), a statement of purpose prepared by the committee.

that injure reputation; (2) withdrawing the conditional privilege from false statements contained in reports of legislative proceedings and on other occasions of privilege; (3) making last minute attacks on a candidate's reputation actionable; and (4) granting candidates the right of reply.

Several states have already enacted measures that incorporate the first of these suggestions. Wisconsin election law, for example, prohibits a false statement "in relation to any candidate, which statement is intended or tends to affect any voting at any election."[8] With minor variations in language, the same provision appears in the corrupt practices acts of Massachusetts, Oregon, Utah, and West Virginia.

In several respects such statutes offer greater protection for both candidates and the public than does the law of defamation. Unlike the latter, they define as offenses not only false statements that reflect on a candidate's character and morality, but also those that misrepresent his voting record, political or personal affiliations, or opinions on issues.[9] They make it possible for the plaintiff or prosecutor to proceed against oral and written false statements with an equal chance for a favorable verdict.[10] They are not actions for damages, and questions concerning the true value of the plaintiff's reputation—questions that make a libel action politically risky—therefore do not arise.

In one particular the application of these laws is narrower than that of the defamation law in cases involving candidates. The laws limit liability to those who "knowingly" make false statements about candidates or who "knowingly"

[8] Wisconsin Statutes (1953), 12.17.

[9] *State ex. rel. Hampel* v. *Mitten,* 278 N.W. 431 (1938).

[10] *Ibid.* The reasonableness of the distinction between libel and slander has become more and more a matter of controversy, with the advent of motion pictures, radio, and television. For an able discussion of this issue, see Richard C. Donnelly, "The Law of Defamation: Proposals for Reform," *Minnesota Law Review* (May 1949), pp. 609-33.

violate the statutory provision. Such a rule puts a heavy burden of proof on the plaintiff—too heavy a burden, if the law is to have a real impact on the conduct of campaigns. If it were changed to make false statements actionable as such, however (as they now are in the state of Michigan), and if certain changes were made in enforcement procedures, such a statute would do a good deal to remedy the weaknesses of existing law.

Withdrawing the conditional privilege from false statements contained in reports of legislative and other government proceedings, when these are published during campaigns, would be a second way to discourage the defamation of candidates. The legal status of such statements has been noted in the preceding chapter: A defamed candidate has recourse against them in a suit for libel only if he can prove malice. Thus false and defamatory materials can be planted in legislative proceedings and on other occasions of absolute privilege for later use in campaigns with little chance that those doing so can be successfully prosecuted. The conditional privilege has been justified by the courts as necessary if citizens are to inform themselves "as to the mode in which a public duty is performed."[11] There could hardly be any subject of greater public interest than the actions and qualifications of candidates for public office, however, and if defamatory false statements made about candidates on other occasions are actionable—as they are in a majority of the states—it is difficult to see why those in reports of public proceedings should not be.

A third measure that holds promise as a way of discouraging unfair attacks on candidates—making last minute charges actionable—has a precedent in the election law of the State of Florida. The relevant statute makes unlawful any attack on a

[11] *Cowley* v. *Pulsifer*, 137 Massachusetts 192 (1884).

115

candidate in the final eighteen days of a campaign unless charges have been personally served on him before that time.[12] Without restricting the debate of personal issues as such, the act attempts to ensure that candidates who are attacked will have the time and opportunity to reply. The requirement of advance notice seems a basically sound way to achieve that purpose, if supported by adequate enforcement procedures.

The Florida statute could, however, be improved in several respects. The Florida Supreme Court has given it a narrow interpretation, holding that it was intended to combat secretly circulated last minute attacks and had "no reference to oral statements or addresses commonly referred to as campaign speeches delivered in a public forum, whether by medium of the voice or by the means of electrical devices."[13] Such a construction reduces the law to relative insignificance. That a fanfare of publicity may accompany a last minute attack in no way ensures that its victim will have adequate time to prepare and distribute an answer. A statute of this kind should be clearly applicable to last minute charges by whatever means communicated.

As it now stands, the statute also gives an unnecessarily vague description of the offense it defines. It prohibits all "charges" and "attacks" made without advance notice in the

[12] In the words of the statute itself, "It shall be unlawful for any candidate or other person, during the eighteen days preceding the day of any election to publish or circulate or cause to be published or circulated any charge against or attack against any candidate unless such charge or attack has been personally served upon the candidate at least eighteen days prior to the day of election, and any person failing to comply with this section shall, upon conviction, be guilty of a misdemeanor. Any answer to a charge or attack that contains defensive matter shall not be construed to be a charge or attack." Florida Statutes (1955), sec. 104-34.

[13] Ex parte Hawthorne, 116 Florida 608 (1934). On the same occasion the court upheld the constitutionality of the law as a reasonable exercise of the police power, not in contravention of the free speech provisions of the Florida Constitution nor of the Fourteenth Amendment of the Constitution of the United States.

last eighteen days of a campaign. The words "charges" and "attacks" seem far too indefinite in meaning for use in a penal statute.[14] The substitution of some phrase having a relatively fixed meaning in law—for example, "attacks upon honesty, integrity, or moral character"—would overcome this objection.

A fourth approach to the control of unfair personal attacks in campaigns would be to grant candidates the right of reply. Right of reply laws involve a principle similar to that embodied in Section 315 of the Federal Communications Act, allowing anyone who is dissatisfied with a newspaper's account of his activities to claim equal space for an answer. Originally a French invention, the right of reply has been given favorable attention by several American legal scholars as an alternative to libel actions in cases of defamation.[15]

The right of reply is currently made available to candidates by statutes in Florida, Mississippi, and Nevada. Of the three statutes, that of Nevada is the most suitable as a model for further legislation of this kind. Under its provisions, the right can be claimed by anyone "named or otherwise designated in such a manner as to be identified," provided he does so within one week after the publication of the objectionable story, if it appears in a daily newspaper, or within thirty days, if it appears in a weekly or periodical. The publisher who receives the reply must carry it in the next issue of his publication, unless this occurs less than two days after receipt, in which case he must publish it in one of the two succeeding issues. He must give the reply "a like position and space and as much display as had the statement which provoked it" and publish it free of charge unless it exceeds the length of the

---

[14] In essence, this was the criticism of the statute made by Justice Buford in a dissenting opinion in the Hawthorne case.

[15] See, for example, Richard C. Donnelly, "The Right of Reply: An Alternative to an Action for Libel," *Virginia Law Review* (November 1948), pp. 867-900; and Zechariah Chafee, Jr., *Government and Mass Communications* (1947), Vol. I, pp. 145-95.

original. An editor refusing to print a reply can be fined and imprisoned.[16]

The right of reply has not been overused in Nevada, and it would be unlikely to impose any severe burden on editors elsewhere, particularly if its operation were limited to candidates for public office. The number of persons entitled to claim the right would be small. Candidates would most probably insist on compliance only in those cases where the treatment given them by a newspaper has been flagrantly unfair and consistently hostile. They would have little to gain, politically, and something to lose if they exercised the right in any other circumstances. To do so would be to risk angering friendly or neutral newspapers, and while the right of reply can be a partial remedy for biased reporting, it can never be a substitute for the present practices that reputable newspapers voluntarily adhere to, that is, to carry answers to attacks in the same story in which an attack is reported.

Within such limits, however, the right of reply offers a candidate accused of misconduct several advantages that existing remedies lack. He can put his reply before the public when the attack is hot. Insofar as it is possible in mass communication, he can direct his answer to the audience before which a charge was given currency. He has recourse not only against false statements, but against distortions of any kind. The remedy is inexpensive, for if the publisher complies, it is not necessary even to hire an attorney, and if the case goes to court, the issues to be decided remain simple ones.

This last feature of the right of reply is one of two that, from the point of view of the public, recommend it. Courts need not concern themselves with the complex questions that a libel case almost always involves. They must consider only whether or not the publication named the complaining party, and whether or not the publisher refused to print a properly

---

[16] Nevada Compiled Laws (1929), sec. 10506.

presented reply. They need not determine whether the statements complained of are true or false or whether their publication was malicious. The other, and principal, advantage that such laws have to offer voters is, of course, greater assurance that they will hear both sides of personal issues.

Taken singly, each of the measures just discussed would leave candidates without protection from many kinds of unfair tactics that have been a part of personal attacks in campaigns. Taken together, however, they would significantly broaden the protection he would receive. They would do so, that is, if ways can be found to make them enforceable and to encourage their enforcement. Only in the case of the right of reply is this not a serious problem in making effective the intent of the law.

Enforcement

If neither a civil suit for damages nor ordinary criminal prosecution offers any reasonable promise of being an effective enforcement procedure for laws designed to curb unfair attacks on candidates, legislators will have to look beyond these conventional methods. Three alternative procedures that deserve their consideration are: (1) allowing courts to enjoin the repetition of false statements about candidates; (2) making violations of such laws grounds for a civil suit to void the election of any candidate violating them; and (3) enabling citizens or groups of citizens to by-pass elected prosecutors and to initiate criminal proceedings in election cases on their own behalf. The first two measures would help to make legal action by candidates a politically feasible course of action, as suits for defamation often are not. The third would help to put in the hands of nonpartisan groups interested in protecting the integrity of elections effective instruments with which to do so.

The first of these suggestions is presently a feature of English law. In the parliamentary elections of that country, any person making or publishing "any false statement of fact in relation to the personal character or conduct" of a candidate may be restrained by injunction "from any repetition of such false statement or any false statement of a similar character."[17] The injunction may be either temporary or perpetual. For the former, prima facie proof of the falsity of the statement is sufficient.

The provision was invoked in the British general election of 1951. The Conservative candidate in East Nottingham, a businessman, was charged by the Labor candidate of an adjoining constituency with having cut his factory's production and laid off workers for political purposes. The Conservative furnished the High Court with evidence of the falsity of the charge and was granted an immediate temporary injunction. The Laborite later retracted his statement and made a full apology. Reporting the incident, David Butler remarked that: "It often happens that no withdrawal ever catches up with an accusation, but in this case very ample publicity was secured, and it was demonstrated that the law could be swift and efficacious in suppressing a canard."[18]

Whether the courts of this country would hold such a procedure constitutional is a question that cannot be answered with certainty, but it is reasonable to assume that they would. It might be argued to the contrary that American courts have consistently held injunctions of future publications unconstitutional, as a prior restraint on speech and publication. The kind of proceeding suggested here, however, does not involve prior restraints—it permits courts to forbid the further circu-

[17] Public General Acts (1895), 58 and 59 Victoria, Chap. 40.
[18] D. E. Butler, *The British General Election of 1951* (1952), p. 32.

lation of words already spoken or published. Such injunction of further circulation has been held not to abridge free speech in a recent decision of the Supreme Court.[19]

What recommends the proceeding as a way of enforcing laws against false statements is its speed. Unlike libel and slander actions, it permits courts to render an authoritative ruling on the truth or falsity of charges before voters go to the polls, and it gives candidates a way to obtain such a ruling at the time that it can have the greatest political impact. Moreover, the courts are unlikely to be plagued by nuisance suits. A candidate who is unable to give good evidence of the falsity of charges against him will hardly care to risk the embarrassment that the refusal of an injunction would entail.

In addition to providing for enforcement in criminal proceedings, the election codes of Wisconsin and Minnesota make false statement laws enforceable by the second procedure noted above—civil suits for the voidance of an election in which violations have occurred. In Wisconsin these may be initiated either by the defeated candidate or by "any elector of the state [who] shall have within his possession information" that the law has been violated.[20] Any successful candidate for a nonlegislative office who has been found guilty of violating the false statement law, or whose personal campaign committee has been guilty of violations, forfeits both his claim to the office he has won and his right to run for it in a new election. If a court finds a candidate for a legislative post guilty of violations, it certifies this finding to the secretary of state for transmission to the presiding officer of

[19] *Kingsley Books, Inc., et al.* v. *Brown,* 354 U.S. 436 (1957). At issue in this case was the constitutionality of a New York statute allowing officials to seek injunctions forbidding the circulation of obscene publications. The court majority held that such a procedure was not restrictive of free speech when the statute "studiously withholds restraint upon matters not already published and not yet found to be offensive."

[20] Wisconsin Statutes (1953), 12.17. The relevant provisions of Minnesota law will be found in Minnesota Election Laws (1956), 211.33-36.

the legislative body for which the violator was a candidate.[21] In effect, therefore, the state has declared it to be public policy that no candidate should enjoy the fruits of a successful campaign if his success depends in any way on a false attack on his opponent.

Politically, an action of the kind just described has a quite different meaning than either a civil suit for defamation or a criminal proceeding. It imposes a political punishment for what is essentially a political offense. It gives the victim of an unfair attack a chance to vindicate himself in a new election. Since such an action is not an action for damages, it may be initiated by a defeated candidate without risking further injury to his reputation or political position from new charges brought against him in the guise of evidence relevant to the assessment of damages. If the action is initiated by a voter— either a disinterested party or a friend of the defeated candidate—such a candidate need not even bear the onus of being a "hard loser."

For all these reasons, the existence of this kind of procedure increases the likelihood that cases arising under false statement laws (the same enforcement procedure could be made applicable also to laws designed to discourage last minute attacks) will in fact be brought to court. This at least seems to have been the case in Wisconsin and Minnesota. The substantive protection afforded candidates by false statement laws in those two states is no greater than that in most states and less than that in some. They have been invoked more often, however, and it seems fair to conclude that the main reason for this is the enforcement procedure by civil suit that they carry, since all cases reported in the two states have been brought to court in that fashion.

It should be noted, however, that both injunctions and the civil suit to void an election have certain limitations that

[21] Wisconsin Statutes (1953), 12.24.

make them, either singly or together, a less than complete answer to the problem of securing the consistent enforcement of laws against unfair attacks. English law restricts the right of judges to enjoin the repetition of false statements to those cases where the statement is so patently false that referring the issue of its truth or falsity to a jury would be superfluous. If it were not so restricted and a jury were employed, the procedure would lose much of the speed that is its principal advantage. Civil suits to void elections, though an effective way to penalize a successful candidate for unfair tactics, cannot be used to punish a defeated one or those carrying on independent campaign activities. In any case, voiding an election can be too severe a punishment for some kinds of offenses.

The third enforcement procedure mentioned at the beginning of this section—enabling citizens to initiate quasi-criminal proceedings—should therefore be considered as a supplement to injunctions and civil suits. Such a procedure would have a precedent in the elections inquest proceeding described by the Massachusetts Corrupt Practices Act. In that state a voter alleging that reasonable grounds exist for believing that certain provisions of the election laws have been violated may file complaint with a district court. The court may then on its own initiative inquire into the alleged violation, summoning and disciplining witnesses as in a criminal case. If it finds the law to have been violated in fact, it reports this conclusion to the superior court, together with the names of persons found guilty of violations.[22] There would seem to be no reason that violations of false statement laws and anti-last-minute attack laws could not be subjected to an inquest of this kind.

It could be argued that to do so would flood the courts with cases, but this objection—one that can be made to any new definition of legal rights—is hardly compelling. A clearly

[22] General Laws of Massachusetts, Chap. 55, secs. 30-36.

drawn statute that is enforceable tends, in and of itself, to reduce the frequency of the offenses it prohibits, since men tend
to refrain from doing that which they know is likely to bring
punishment. Moreover, in advising clients, members of the
bar do a great deal to discourage nuisance suits. If such
natural protections against unjustified litigation should prove
inadequate, standard measures could be taken to discourage
it.

Assuming that there is a desire to see legal controls on unfair personal attacks made effective, the case for an inquest
enforcement procedure can be summed up in a few words. It
would allow citizen groups to play an active role in policing
campaigns and would make it possible for them to take action
against anyone committing offenses defined by law, whether
the offender is a candidate or not. Just as new laws are necessary if citizen groups are to act effectively against unfair campaign practices, therefore, so is the growth of groups interested in combating such practices necessary to effective law
enforcement.

Summary

This chapter and the preceding one have been concerned
with some of the shortcomings of the discussion of personal
issues in political campaigns. These shortcomings are not basically different in kind from those of policy discussion, but
they have somewhat different consequences and are amenable
to somewhat different methods of control. In principle the
discussion of personal issues has always been held within
stricter limits than that of policy issues; this has been true
mainly in principle, however, for existing controls or abuses,
both legal and nonlegal, have been largely ineffective.

An examination of the reasons for this state of affairs suggests additional measures that could be taken by the press, citizen groups, and legislators to change it. Newspapers and the broadcast media, bound by overly rigid interpretations of objectivity, have too often permitted themselves to become common carriers for campaign smears. Not only should they give full and equal coverage to attacks and replies, they should take the initiative in gathering and presenting all the information relevant to assessing the accuracy of accusations and should feel free to use silence as a weapon against last minute attacks.

The electorate, treated too long to campaigns where questionable tactics have been used by both sides, has tended to accept such tactics as "a part of the game." This attitude, which encourages campaigners to live up (or down) to the electorate's expectations, can be countered in part by citizen group action similar to that now carried on by the Fair Campaign Practices Committee. Citizens groups can help build a public demand for fair campaigning by directing the public's attention to the nature of smear tactics and to the extent of 'heir use. As the F.C.P.C. has shown, there are a wide variety of publicity techniques available to them in pursuing these objectives.

The laws governing the discussion of candidates in campaigns have been too meager in the substantive protection they extend and too poorly enforced to be an effective curb on unfair campaign practices. They have been poorly enforced because enforcement has waited on action either by elected public prosecutors or on candidates who take their cases to court only at considerable political risk. The substantive protection given candidates could be broadened by making all politically injurious false statements actionable, by withdrawing the conditional privilege during campaigns, by making last minute attacks actionable, and by granting candidates the right of reply. Enforcement of anti-smear statutes could be made more certain by establishing procedures that would allow courts to enjoin the repetition of false statements about candidates, that would enable candidates or voters to bring civil suits to void elections where violations occur, and that would permit citizens to initiate election inquests.

7

Identifying Communicators

THE PRESENT CHAPTER will examine some factors that impair the electorate's ability to get accurate information about the sources of campaign communication. This is the intended effect of some common campaign practices and the consequence of others. Both kinds of practices raise questions of public policy, the existing answers to which are less than satisfactory. Before reviewing these, however, it may be useful to state again, as precisely as possible, just what voters need to know about the sources of campaign statements, and why they need to know it.

First, it is important for voters to know who is saying what in campaigns because such knowledge is needed to assign value and meaning to campaign communications. The political significance of a communication is as dependent on its authorship as on its substance. A statement by a candidate may mean one thing, the same statement by a supporter quite another. Moreover, some knowledge of the source of a communication is, in many cases, a prerequisite to judging its reliability. This is not to say that the truth of a statement depends on its authorship. It is to say that voters frequently are not in a position to test the validity of statements against their experience or by observation, and they must therefore act on the assumption that there is a positive correlation between the reliability of a statement and its author's record for reliability. The electorate, like a court, must frequently rely on the testimony of witnesses in determining what has or has not happened, and, consequently, must examine the credibility of the witnesses in assigning a value to such testimony.[1]

A second reason that the electorate's knowledge of the sources of campaign communication is important is that variations in such knowledge affect the content of campaign statements. Communicators know that they will be judged by what they say. When the electorate is unable to identify them, therefore, they will show less responsibility in their communications. The ventriloquist is humble in his opinions, but his dummy delights in outrageous statements.

Thus, provided one makes clear the meaning of the word "knowledge," there should be little disagreement with the proposition that the ability of voters to respond rationally to campaign communication depends on their knowledge of its sources. In the present discussion, the following kinds of information about sources are assumed to be essential to the valid interpretation of a communication: (1) The name, or some other identifying characteristic, of the communicator; (2) the intent of the communicator, *i.e.*, the nature of his interest in reactions to the communication; and (3) the communicator's record for reliability, or, if he is an agent for someone else, his principal's record for reliability. Access to such information, may, for the reasons just given, be considered a condition necessary for the rationality of electoral decisions. In campaigns this condition is most obviously violated by the circulation of anonymous publications.

[1] John Locke has stated as concisely as anyone, perhaps, the grounds on which we judge the probable truth of a statement. These are, "First, the conformity of anything with our own knowledge, observation, and experience. Secondly, the testimony of others vouching their observation and experience." In assessing the latter, he observes that it should be given more or less credit according to its consistency; the circumstances under which it has been offered; the presence or absence of contrary testimony; and the number, integrity, skill, and designs of the witnesses. "An Essay Concerning Human Understanding," in Edwin A. Burtt (ed.), *The English Philosophers from Bacon to Mill* (1939), p. 379.

The Politics of Anonymity

The circulation of anonymous literature has been a persistent and frequent practice in contests for office in the United States. Some notion of the dimensions it may assume emerges from the report of a Senate Special Committee that surveyed campaign tactics in the presidential race of 1940.[2] Of four hundred specimens of allegedly vicious and scurrilous publications collected by the committee, about one third were anonymous and one half either anonymous or insufficiently identified.[3] Although many of these appear to have been the work of isolated individuals in particular localities, both the character and wide distribution of others suggest that they were a part of some over-all plan of campaign.

Hugh Bone, in a book based on this Senate committee's findings, identifies two forms of anonymous literature: that which bears no identification whatsoever and that issued under assumed names, *e.g.,* "A Willkie Booster" or "Patriot." To these may be added a third: that in which the source is falsely identified. This latter type of anonymous literature was used during the presidential campaign of 1956. Letters postmarked Atlanta, Georgia, and purporting to come from the "Council of White Citizens of Atlanta," were sent to some 6,000 Negro voters in Detroit, Michigan, urging them to vote Democratic "because the Democratic Party keeps the colored in their place."[4] The Council of White Citizens of Atlanta was a fictitious organization. The letters had actually been

[2] *Investigation of Presidential, Vice Presidential, and Senatorial Campaign Expenditures, 1940,* S. Rept. 47, 77 Cong. 1 sess.

[3] *Ibid.,* pp. 14-15.

[4] *Washington Post and Times Herald,* Jan. 9, 1957.

sent by John R. McAlpine, a Detroit advertising man who did volunteer work for the Michigan Minutemen for Eisenhower.[5]

From Bone's study it would appear that the anonymous publication serves as a medium for several kinds of appeals, and the relationship between these appeals and the irresponsibility conferred by anonymity seems quite clear. Libelous attacks on the candidates were frequent. President Roosevelt was likened to Benedict Arnold and Wendell Willkie was represented as a friend of Nazi Germany. There were occasional mixtures of politics and obscenity. Most common of all, perhaps, were what might be called "bootleg appeals"—appeals that no candidate or party committee could have made directly without alienating support. The most conspicuous examples were the numerous pieces that attempted to exploit racial and religious prejudices.

Several generalizations about the impact of anonymous publications on electoral decisions seem plausible, although there exists little exact information by which one might assess it. Since the appeals of most such literature are "obvious, naive, and superficial,"[6] the effect of anonymous literature is probably greatest among the most gullible members of the electorate. Rational men would normally disregard it, although they might easily be misled by literature the source of which is falsely identified, and those who circulate anonymous publications may also count on the fact that a message may linger in the mind after the recipient of the message has forgotten that its source was untrustworthy.[7] Whatever the magnitude of the tendency of anonymous publication to subvert electoral rationality, however, that it tends to do so would seem open to little question.

[5] *Ibid.*

[6] Hugh A. Bone, "Smear" Politics: An analysis of the 1940 campaign literature (1941), p. 33.

[7] For experimental evidence on this phenomenon see Carl I. Hovland and Walter Weiss, "The Influence of Source Credibility on Communication," *Public Opinion Quarterly* (Winter 1951), pp. 635-51.

A second practice in campaigning that impairs the electorate's ability to identify the sources of communication is that of organizing "fronts." For present purposes, a front may be defined as any organization, ostensibly independent, the decisions of which are in fact controlled by another group or organization. An examination of the activities of two fronts in the campaigns of 1950 gives an indication of how they work and the uses to which they may be put in the dissemination of propaganda.

In the Ohio senatorial campaign, a group that called itself "Farmers for Ferguson" sponsored several pieces of literature distributed among farmers in that state. Manifestly, it was a farmer organization—its officers were farmers who had long been identified with the Democratic party. In fact, a group of labor unions were wholly responsible for the preparation, financing, and circulation of the literature distributed under the organization's name. The farmers' functions were apparently limited to reading and approving this literature and to masking the identity of its real sponsors.[8]

The Maryland senatorial campaign of 1950 saw a front organization used as the sponsor of one of the most controversial pieces of campaign literature in recent years. This was the tabloid, already referred to,[9] which included the composite photograph of Senator Millard Tydings and Communist leader Earl Browder. The tabloid advertised its sponsors as "Young Democrats for Butler, Edward B. Freeman, Chairman; John B. Purnell, Treasurer." Some 300,000 copies were distributed by mail and by hand in the last week of the campaign.

The "Young Democrats" were a legally constituted committee of some six registered Democratic voters. They had no

[8] See *Investigation into the 1950 Ohio Senatorial Campaign*, Hearings before the Senate Committee on Rules and Administration, 82 Cong. 1 and 2 sess., pp. 274-79.
[9] Chap. 5, p. 89.

affiliation with any regular young Democratic organization. They met only twice. The chairman of the group disclaimed any advance notice of the tabloid's preparation or distribution. Its treasurer gave approval for the use of the organization's name as sponsor of the tabloid, but seems never to have been consulted regarding its content. This was in fact controlled by staff members of the *Washington Times Herald,* some members of the late Senator Joseph R. McCarthy's staff, and by Republican candidate John M. Butler's campaign manager. The costs of printing and distribution were likewise borne by Butler's campaign organization. The Senate Subcommittee on Privileges and Elections, reporting its investigation of the campaign, alleged that sponsorship of the tabloid by the Young Democrats for Butler constituted a violation of the federal and state laws requiring persons responsible for such publications to list the organization and its officers.[10] Whether or not a technical violation of these laws was involved, however, the Butler campaign organization had clearly succeeded in circumventing their intent, and it is fair to say that the Young Democrats for Butler was an organization in name only, serving as sponsor in name only of propaganda emanating from other sources.[11]

From these two examples, one may conclude that fronts serve essentially the same purposes as anonymity, though more subtly—certainly any other conclusion would seem forced. They tend, and are intended, to mislead voters by creating the impression that a candidate is receiving widespread and independent support, by hiding the partisan interests behind particular campaign appeals, and by propagating appeals that a candidate could not make without risk of back-

---

[10] *Maryland Senatorial Election of 1950,* Report of the Senate Committee on Rules and Administration, 82 Cong. 1 sess., p. 4.

[11] For a more complete account of the organization and its activities, see *Maryland Senatorial Election of 1950,* Hearings before the Senate Committee on Rules and Administration, 81 Cong. 2 sess., pp. 348-67.

fire. They do so without simultaneously arousing the same degree of suspicion with which anonymous literature is normally received.

In some respects a more important observation to be made on the two cases just discussed, however, would be this: When one looks at actual campaign organizations, the definition of a front given above is a less useful tool for classifying such organizations than it might at first appear. Both the Farmers for Ferguson and the Young Democrats for Butler were fronts, but not in quite the same way. The officers of the Farmers for Ferguson seem to have had a veto power (though an unexercised one) over the content of the material they sponsored. The Young Democrats for Butler cannot really be said to have exercised even this much control over the use of the organization's name. This kind of difference has little significance in itself, but it suggests some questions. Suppose that the Farmers for Ferguson had prepared their own material, relying on the unions only for the financing of its distribution. Could they still have been called a front? Would they have been a front if they had received only a part of their financial support from labor unions? Is it possible, in short, to define any precise point at which an organization becomes a front for interests outside itself?

The answer would seem to be "no," not without being more or less arbitrary. In a significant sense, all campaign organizations are fronts; all speak for some combination of interests the composition of which is not immediately knowable. It is only true in part that "the public knows pretty well where each political party stands, and what each represents. They present no great problem of mislabeling and misbranding."[12] In reality, the character of the groups that direct party committees, and of the interests they represent, changes

---

[12] *Campaign Expenditures,* Report of the Special Committee to Investigate Campaign Expenditures, H. Rept. 2093, 78 Cong. 2 sess., p. 7.

over time. It is to some extent by convention only that we speak of Republican or Democratic headquarters in successive campaigns as if we were referring to the same two groups.

Partly because their relationship to candidates is almost always somewhat ambiguous, party committees sometimes behave rather like organizations that are more obviously fronts. As has already been observed, the literature issued by party committees for mass circulation is often characterized by appeals more blatant than the candidate himself could afford to make. This was true, for instance, in the case of the Republican National Committee comic book that represented recent wars as "Democratic Wars," a charge which President Eisenhower subsequently had to disavow. The normal ambiguity of the candidate-committee relationship allows a kind of division of labor between them. The committees may sponsor appeals which, if effective, will benefit the candidate, but for which, if they backfire, the candidate cannot be held responsible.

That all campaign organizations have some of the characteristics and consequences of fronts becomes even more obvious if one considers the impact on campaign communication of the ensemble of groups that seek to persuade voters. The amount of literature distributed by nonparty groups in any given campaign is probably as great as, or greater than, that distributed by the parties.[13] This is certainly not anonymous literature in any technical sense. Nor are most such organizations formed with any intent to deceive the voter. Some are formed to circumvent the legal restrictions on campaign spending. Some are the instruments of a party faction that is at odds with the regular organization. Many, perhaps most, are in effect auxiliaries of regular party organizations with a specialized campaign task—to raise money, sponsor a rally,

[13] On this point see Bone, *op. cit.,* p. 6.

or appeal to some particular group in the electorate. A few are entirely nonpolitical in inspiration, devoted solely to the enrichment of their organizers through the solicitation of campaign funds.

Yet, viewed realistically, the communications sponsored by most of the organizations active in campaigns are quasi-anonymous, since voters can discover only with difficulty the interests and reliability of those who direct their activities. This is true if only because there are so many organizations sponsoring campaign communications and so many of these exist only during the campaign. A study of the New Jersey gubernatorial campaign of 1957[14] found thirteen organizations, not counting the two parties, campaigning on behalf of candidates Robert Meyner and Malcolm Forbes. Of these, only five could be called permanent organizations. The remaining eight had been formed at the beginning of the campaign, disbanded as soon as it was over, and had no regular qualifications for members or procedures for accepting them. Clearly, the name of one of these organizations on a piece of campaign literature could tell the voter almost nothing about its character, reputation, or relation to the candidate.

Thus, it is not deceptive practices alone that make it difficult for voters to acquire information about the sources of campaign communication; it is difficult for them to do so partly because of the sheer complexity of the process of campaign communication. Knowledge of the sources of communication varies with the scope of the communications system. In small face-to-face groups that remain in existence for some time, the liar, the alarmist, and the self-interested pleader develop reputations as such. In a mass society, communicators may speak with many voices and under many

[14] A study made by a graduate research seminar of the Woodrow Wilson School of Public and International Affairs (of Princeton University) and financed by the Carnegie Corporation of New York. The project was directed by Professor Richard Frost of Princeton University and by the author.

names, and recipients of communication must react somewhat as they would at a masquerade ball—hopefully, distrust-
fully, noncommittally.

Problems of Control

The preceding discussion of the problems that confront
voters in establishing the character of sources of communication raises two questions for those concerned with the contributions of campaigning to electoral rationality: What measures can be taken to discourage attempts to mislead voters
by failures to identify or by mis-identification of the sources
of communication? What measures can be taken to ensure
or to help ensure that voters will receive relevant information
about the sources of communication? A brief review of the
responses legislators have given to these questions will suggest some of the shortcomings of existing answers and some
of the problems involved in answering them.

Laws prohibiting the circulation of anonymous literature
in campaigns have been one such response. The federal government and most of the states have enacted such statutes.
Federal law makes it a crime to publish, distribute, mail, or
transport in interstate commerce any statement relating to
candidates for federal office, unless such a statement carries
with it the "names of the persons, associations, committees,
or corporations responsible for the publication or distribution of the same."[15] Most of the state laws on the subject
carry similar provisions.

Undoubtedly, such laws deter anonymous publication to
some extent. Newspapers and printers, particularly, are apt
to be hesitant to become involved in violations of them.

[15] U.S. Code, Title 18, sec. 612.

Nonetheless, it should be apparent that they offer only a limited answer to the general problem under discussion here. For one thing, while there have been prosecutions for violation of these statutes, it is doubtful that they have been enforced consistently. For another, they are no solution to the problem of fronts and the quasi-anonymity such organizations confer.

The nearest approach legislators have made to the latter problem is to pass laws requiring campaign organizations to report the names of financial contributors. The Federal Corrupt Practices Act presently requires certain specified committees to report at stated intervals the names and addresses of all persons making contributions of $100 or more. The act also stipulates that a person making an expenditure in excess of $50 during a calendar year for the purpose of influencing elections in two or more states (except when the expenditure takes the form of a contribution to a political committee) must file a statement of such an expenditure. Most state election codes also require the reporting of contributions, with differing provisions as to what contributions are to be reported by whom, in what form, and when. Though it has been of varying effect and effectiveness, such legislation does show an appreciation of the fact that voters need to know more than the names of those who sponsor communications if they are to assign meaning to campaign statements. They must also be given some indication of the interests that support particular candidacies and committees.

The principal shortcomings of such laws, as they have operated in practice, are well known. Contributions are often reported in such a manner—without summaries, without segregation of loans and contributions, and in such great detail—that a meaningful analysis of them is difficult to make. Often reports are not filed before elections and are little publicized when filed, making them of little value to voters in arriving at voting decisions. Enforcement has been lax in the extreme—the Federal Corrupt Practices Act fails even to designate an official responsible for examining reports and referring violations to the Attorney General.

Experience with such laws does suggest, however, some of the requirements that measures designed to increase the voter's knowledge of the sources of communication should meet. They should attempt to make available all information about communicators—or as much information as it is possible to make available—that is relevant to the interpretation of the communications they sponsor. To require communicators to reveal the names of those who finance their activities by no means exhausts what might be done to this end; the role of money in politics should not become an *idée fixe*. How to broaden the substantive requirements for information in laws governing the activities of campaign organizations, then, is one problem that must be faced by those interested in the enactment of such laws.

Adequate law enforcement procedures are a second problem that must be solved if legislation is to prove of any value in alleviating the voter's informational problems. In part, this means finding ways to overcome the resistance to consistent enforcement that is evident in the case of criminal statutes prohibiting false statements about candidates. Politically elected prosecutors often have something to lose and little to gain if they take enforcement duties too seriously. In part it means developing methods for coping with the sheer magnitude of the enforcement problem. Campaign organizations spring up, proliferate, and disappear in the space of a few weeks or months.

Finally, there must not only be information to publicize, but it must actually be publicized in such ways and at such times as to enable it to influence votes. How best to ensure such publication is, of course, one of the questions that the authors of laws requiring organizations to report contributions and expenditures have too often failed to consider. Press performance in this regard must also be rated as unsatisfactory. Frequently the press has let itself be used by the sponsors of front organizations to convey the impression that the sponsors of such organizations want to convey, namely, that they are independent, substantial, and spontaneous movements.

Approaches to Solution

It is much easier to show the difficulties of the problem being considered here and to outline an ideal solution for it, than it is to suggest measures that would in fact solve it. One can, however, show ways to make it a less urgent problem, and, if this is the objective, five measures deserve special attention: (1) press features on the activities of non-party campaign organizations and the interpretive reporting of such activities; (2) a revision of the laws prohibiting the circulation of anonymous literature; (3) a requirement that candidates approve or disapprove all literature circulated on their behalf; (4) a disclosure of information statute; and (5) a requirement that the buying of space and time from the media of communication, purchase of the services of printers, and use of the mails for campaign purposes be made conditional on the disclosure of information about the sponsor of the proposed communication.

Reference has already been made to how inadequately many newspapers handle the activities of non-party campaign organizations. The typical news release of such an organization is calculated to impress voters with the organization's independence of regular party organizations, and editors too often fail to go behind such claims to give their readers an appreciation of what seems normally to be the true state of affairs: that such organizations exist more on paper than in reality; that their officers are persons with long standing partisan or interest group affiliations; and that the communications of such organizations are cleared by the candidate's publicity or public relations director. If background information on the character of such groups were introduced into news reports of their campaign statements, these would be much less misleading. Feature stories on the auxiliary organizations active in particular campaigns would also be a useful addition to the flow of information that goes to voters.

There are probably two main reasons the press often fails to report information of this kind: a narrow interpretation of "objectivity" in news reporting and the cost of collecting it. The latter reason would seem to be at least as important as the former. It could be made considerably less compelling if auxiliary organizations were required by law to disclose information that would indicate the nature of the interests they represent and their relations with candidates and party committees, and if this information were made easily accessible to the press. Some recent changes in the Florida law on the reporting of contributions, for instance—including simplified reporting forms—seem to have generated a great deal of publicity on this particular aspect of campaigning. In the words of one observer, "The publicity which was necessary if the law was to be meaningful was provided by a conscientious corps of political reporters, including representatives of both Associated and United Press, who eagerly awaited the arrival of the official reports at the Secretary of State's office in order to send an account of the contents to their respective offices for publication."[16] Here, once again, it seems clear that legal and nonlegal measures could usefully supplement each other.

[16] Elston E. Roady, "Florida's New Campaign Expense Law and the 1952 Democratic Gubernatorial Primaries," *American Political Science Review*, Vol. 48 (June 1954), pp. 475-76.

A revision of the laws prohibiting the circulation of anonymous literature has been mentioned as one legal measure that might be taken. While the best of such statutes goes but a little way toward giving voters the information about communication sources they need, they are nonetheless a step in that direction, and those of some states could be made more effective than they are presently. A model statute of this kind should apply to all matter, in whatever form published, that tends to affect voting in any election. It should require that such material carry the name of the sponsoring organization, its address, and the names of the organization's officers and their addresses. The laws of several states fail to require communicators to furnish their addresses, and these are an important part of any law designed to discourage anonymous publication, since they make fictitious names easier to detect. Some also fail to require the name of the printer to appear on literature, thus depriving enforcement officials of another aid in the detection of violators. Remedying some of these common deficiencies would strengthen state laws on this subject.

The third measure noted above—requiring candidates to approve or disapprove all communications distributed in their behalf—has a precedent in the laws of Mississippi and was a feature of a recent Senate bill introduced as an amendment to the Federal Corrupt Practices Act.[17] The Mississippi statute (which applies only to primary campaigns) provides that:

> No person shall write, print, post, or distribute or cause to be distributed, a notice, placard, bill, poster, dodger, pamphlet, advertisement or any other form of publication (except notices, posters, and the like, which simply announce a speaking date and invite attendance thereon) which is designed to influence voters for or against any candidate at a primary, unless and until the same shall have been submitted to, and approved and subscribed by the candidate or by his campaign manager or assistant

[17] S. 1437, 85 Cong. 1 sess., introduced by Senator Albert Gore of Tennessee.

manager, which subscription shall in all cases be printed as so subscribed, and not otherwise.[18]

The Senate bill cited above was less restrictive in intent. It would not have forbidden political committees to circulate literature without authorization, but it would have required them to give notice of their lack of authorization if they had failed to obtain it.[19]

What could be expected from a measure of this kind? Obviously, it would give voters some indication of the relationship between candidates and those who issue statements soliciting support for them—a datum that they need to interpret such statements accurately. It should also tend to discourage the organization of fronts—particularly if it followed the Mississippi model—for there would be little advantage in organizing a front if responsibility for its statements were placed squarely on the candidate whom it had been organized to support. Finally, since such a measure would place the responsibility for campaign statements on candidates, it would tend to discourage bootleg appeals and, to some extent perhaps, libelous attacks.[20]

About the practicality of requiring candidates to authorize campaign statements, there would appear to be little question; Mississippi politicians questioned by the author had found that the law imposed no great burden either on them or their

[18] Mississippi Code Annotated of 1942, 3176.

[19] In the words of the bill: "No political committee shall print or publish any card, pamphlet, circular, poster, dodger, sticker, advertisement, book, writing or other statement in support of any specific candidate who has not authorized such committee to support his candidacy, without stating thereon in letters of such size as to be easily legible that such committee has not been authorized by such candidate to support his candidacy." S. 1437, 85 Cong. 1 sess., Title II, sec. 202 (f).

[20] The author questioned members of Mississippi's congressional delegation, the State's Attorney General, and a number of its political party officials about the provision. All those who responded, nine in all, felt that it had helped to discourage irresponsible campaign statements and that it was generally observed.

campaign managers. The constitutionality of a law prohibiting the circulation of campaign literature without authorization is less certain, although this objection could not be raised against a requirement that unauthorized literature be designated as such. The Mississippi statute has never been challenged on constitutional grounds, and there has been, therefore, no authoritative determination of this issue. There might be some question, finally, as to the desirability of applying the stricter provisions of the Mississippi statutes to presidential nominating contests, in which independent committees may be formed to promote the draft of a non-candidate. The enactment of the Gore bill, however, would seem to erect no real obstacles to drafts.

A disclosure of information statute—a fourth measure that might be taken to increase the electorate's knowledge of the sources of campaign communication—should include provisions that would require the reporting of campaign contributions, but it should go beyond this to require the reporting of other information as well. At the very least, this additional information should include: (1) the names and addresses of the persons or organizations sponsoring any given campaign statement; (2) the names and addresses of the officers of any such organization; (3) the date on which the organization was formed; (4) a statement of the organization's purpose; (5) qualifications for membership in the organization, if any; (6) the number of members in the organization; (7) the scope of the organization's operations, that is, whether national, state, or local; and (8) whether or not the organization has a charter and by-laws. For such a statute to be useful, of course, definitions of such terms as "membership" would have to be carefully drawn.

The administration of such a statute might well be modeled on Florida's "Who Gave It—Who Got It" law. This requires all individuals, committees, and organizations expending any money on behalf of any candidate to file reports with the Office of the Secretary of State at regular intervals during an election campaign. Florida legislators, as it has already been noted, deliberately avoided over-elaborate reports in order to get one that would lend itself to easy analysis, and their example would seem a good one to follow. A change in the scope of the law that should perhaps be considered would be to make it applicable to any person, group, or organization sponsoring communications intended or tending to affect voting, rather than limiting its application to those spending money in support of particular candidacies.

The primary intent of such a statute, of course, would be to make information on the character of campaign organizations available for publication. Government could take a more active role in encouraging publicity by printing data taken from the reports and distributing it to newspaper editors, radio and television news staffs, candidates, and party committees. Realization of the statute's intent, however, would depend in large part on how and whether candidates and news media used the information the reports would provide.

It would depend also on how well the law was enforced. If consistent enforcement is desired, a disclosure of information statute should not only be enforceable in ordinary criminal proceedings but also by election inquests, since the problems of securing enforcement would be similar to those that attend laws designed to discourage unfair attacks on candidates. Another way to help ensure compliance would be to make such compliance a necessary condition of the right to buy time and space for campaign statements in the communication media, or to buy the services of printers or use the mails for that purpose. This final measure of the five, mentioned at the beginning of this section, would put an obligation on printers, publishers, and broadcasters to ascertain whether or not organizations had filed reports, thus locating responsibility in persons who normally have a continuous stake in complying with the law.

Summary

Proceeding on the assumption that voters cannot interpret the substance of campaign communication accurately unless they know its sources, this chapter has outlined some of the conditions on which knowledge of source depends and some of the practices that make these conditions difficult of practical realization. The great numbers of organizations sponsoring campaign communications, their ephemeral nature, the deliberate fostering of front organizations, and the circulation of anonymous literature—all of these impair the ability of the electorate to respond rationally to campaign discussion.

Although the control of such practices is no simple matter, a number of measures would help to control them and to mitigate their effects. Among these would be revision of some of the existing statutes prohibiting the circulation of anonymous literature; a requirement that candidates approve or disapprove literature distributed in support of their candidacies; a disclosure of information statute; a requirement that the right to purchase and sell time and space in the communication media be conditioned on the purchaser's disclosure of certain information about himself or his organization; and better press reporting of the nature, interests, affiliations, and activities of campaign organizations.

8

A Concluding Review

THE PURPOSE OF this final chapter is to review the argument of the preceding pages and, in so doing, to reduce it to its bare bones. Stated concisely, its principal thesis is this: American political campaigns often take forms that make campaign discussion either worthless or misleading as a guide for voters, and this fact cannot be regarded simply as an inevitable consequence of the campaign situation. The contribution of campaign discussion to rationality in voting can be increased by a conscious public policy directed to that end.

The notion that the campaign should help the voter to cast his vote wisely is the ideal function assigned to it in American political thought. To say it does not serve this function well, is to do little more than to state the obvious. Campaign communication is filled with evasions, distortions, ambiguities, irrelevancies, and calculated efforts to mislead. Seemingly, it confirms the proposition that the rational interests of candidates and parties lead them to encourage irrationality in the electorate.[1]

In political commentary there have been a number of reactions to this state of affairs. Some have ignored it, others have condemned it angrily. A few have argued that it makes imperative a less important role for public opinion in the determination of public policy—that decision-makers must be less bound by popular opinion if they are to respond rationally to the

---

[1] *Cf.* Anthony Downs, *An Economic Theory of Democracy* (1957), p. 160.

challenges of the nation's international, economic, and social environment. A few have abandoned, or dismissed, the idea that education can be the social objective of the campaign, attempting to show that campaigns serve other purposes no less useful to society; that, for instance, they are a psychic substitute for physical violence, or that they encourage a sense of popular participation in the actions of government.

One cannot be entirely happy with any of these reactions, for the failure of campaigning to serve an educational function has quite real consequences. The opinions of the electorate, informed or uninformed, rational or irrational, do influence the course of governmental action. The fact of popular sovereignty normally does not mean that government policy mirrors the preferences of an electoral majority. But it does mean, as Robert Dahl has observed, that government must take into account the preferences of a greater variety of larger minorities than it would otherwise.[2] If the members of these powerful minorities hold their opinions irrationally, if the demands they make on government are mere whims or prejudices, it is hardly reasonable to suppose that governmental decisions can have either the stability or the flexibility that a rational response to the problems of government presupposes.

To prescribe measures for increasing the rationality of electoral action would require one to examine all the conditions on which rationality in voting may depend (or all the important ones). The present study has set for itself a much less ambitious project, which, however, would be a part of any such undertaking. Its central concern has been how one significant influence on voting—the discussion of policies and candidates in campaigns—might make a greater contribution to electoral rationality. Since the relevance of this issue to any action in the real world depends on an ability to identify and modify the factors that determine campaign communication, a summary

[2] Robert Dahl, *A Preface to Democratic Theory* (1956), p. 132.

147

statement of those identified or assumed in preceding chapters is perhaps in order.

First, the constitutional status of speech and publication conditions the character of campaign discussion. This fact should be so obvious as to require little comment. Other things being equal, the constitutional protections given speech and publication in the United States encourage the maximum expression of difference of opinion and the greatest diversity in the form such expression takes. They confine the range of possible legal controls on campaign discussion within narrow limits.

Second, the character of a nation's party system is an important determinant of the forms that its political discussion will take. A multiparty system aggravates differences of opinion in the electorate—it creates issues. A two-party system aggregates opinion, and the differences in the policy positions taken by the two parties will normally be moderate. As V. O. Key expresses this idea and draws its implications for American politics:

> Each party leadership must maintain the loyalty of its own standpatters; it must also concern itself with the great blocks of voters uncommitted to either party as well as with those who may be weaned away from the opposition. These influences tend to pull the party leaderships from their contrasting anchorages toward the center. In that process, perhaps most visible in presidential campaigns, the party appeals often sound much alike and thereby contribute to the bewilderment of observers of American politics.[3]

A party system in which power is effectively decentralized, as it has been in the American party system, also has consequences for campaign discussion. Decentralization tends to encourage differences in the policy appeals of candidates of the same party, and discourages, therefore, the development of any but the vaguest of party ideologies. It also encourages a lack

[3] V. O. Key, *Politics, Parties and Pressure Groups* (1958), p. 241.

of discipline in legislative parties, which, in turn, means that public discussion of legislative activities will fail to shape political issues in a way that is directly relevant to choices at the polls.

Third, the electoral system is an important determinant of the character of campaign discussion. Fixed dates for elections, designated by law, mean that in some elections there will be few important issues at stake and low interest in the affairs of government. This encourages campaigners either to manufacture issues or to emphasize personality or party appeals. Similarly, when the electoral system makes the voter's choice one between candidates, rather than party lists, campaign organizations will tend to give greater emphasis to the personal qualities and qualifications of candidates in electoral propaganda. Nominations by primary election have an effect similar to that of party decentralization. They allow dissident factions a better chance to win policy disputes within parties in any given jurisdiction, and thus increase the chances that candidates of the same party will make contrasting appeals to the electorate in general elections.

Fourth, the competitive nature of campaign discussion is an important determinant of the character it assumes. Campaigners, in order to win, must get a greater number of votes than their opponents. For them campaign communication is instrumental, that is, one way to win votes. It is instrumental also in a more limited sense, for even if the participants in campaign discussion do not consider what they say to be purely a means to an end, they are nevertheless already committed to the points of view they express: they use discussion to persuade, not to learn. For both these reasons campaign discussion becomes "a forensic combat between two sides in which the object of each is to defeat the other at the polls" and may bear little resemblance to disinterested discussion where "the object of all participants is to seek the answer to a particular question, namely: What policies are best calculated to advance the *common* welfare and *shared* interests of all members of the community?"[4]

Fifth, the character of campaign discussion is determined, in part, by the character of the electorate. Obviously, much of the content of campaign communication will reflect the interests and concerns of voters, and, where these vary, so will the content of campaign communication. Much of the activity of campaign organizations is devoted to efforts to discovering these interests and concerns so that campaign appeals may be formed accordingly. Differences in the ability of members of the electorate to reason, in their tendency to approach public problems rationally (certainly this is in part a cultural characteristic), in their basic knowledge of public affairs, and in the amount of information they possess will condition the manner in which campaigners present these appeals. One may expect almost all campaign communication to be *ad hominem,* in the sense that it will be tailored to its audience and profoundly shaped by the strengths and weaknesses of that audience.

A trap into which one may easily fall when thinking about the relationship of campaign discussion to the character of the electorate should perhaps be noted here. This is to treat the electorate as if it were homogeneous in composition, and as if its character were adequately described by an average of the characteristics of its members. This tendency has been encouraged both because the findings of most empirical studies have been presented in such terms and because much of campaign discussion is aimed at the largest possible audience. But the electorate is not all of a piece. It is more realistic to speak of electorates than of the electorate. One could distinguish, in the general voting public, an *elite* electorate, composed of

[4] Austin Ranney and Willmoore Kendall, *Democracy and the American Party System* (1956), p. 515.

those party and interest group leaders whose support will be personally solicited; a *partisan* electorate, composed of the great body of party activists; a *quality* electorate—an "informed and interested stratum"[5] attentive to the actions of government and to the development of governmental policies; the *mass* electorate, composed of the great body of voters; and, perhaps, a *gullible* electorate, a group ill qualified to vote, the targets of anonymous literature and whispering campaigns. This way of thinking about the voting public is useful for at least two reasons: it avoids an identification of campaigning designed to arouse the mass electorate with all campaigning; and it is an antidote to the notion that the electorate gets what it deserves. It is quite possible, for instance, that a campaign discussion aimed at the level of the average voter would fail to mobilize the intellectual resources of the community for collective decisions in an optimum manner.

Sixth, the character of those sponsoring communication is an important influence on the character of campaign discussion. What is said in campaigns depends in part on the interests, positions, intelligence, and moral sensibilities of those who say it, and any analysis that neglects to take account of this fact will be a distortion of reality. When campaigners oversimplify issues, it is not always because they think an oversimplified version will win more votes than a complex one. They sometimes see issues in oversimplified terms themselves. Moreover, the politician's internalized sense of what is proper may lead him to eschew certain appeals, though such appeals might be effective, just as the involvement in a competitive situation in the long run tends to shape his sense of what is proper. The nature of the politician's ethic and its consequences for his behavior is a subject that could fruitfully re-

---

[5] Gabriel A. Almond, *The American People and Foreign Policy* (1950), p. 139. The term "quality electorate" was suggested to the author by Professor Almond.

ceive more systematic study. It is probable that, while it would
not coincide with the formal ethic of the general community,
neither would it be a mere rationalization of the politician's
interests in winning power and prestige. As among businessmen there is proper and improper padding of expense accounts, so among politicians there are permissible kinds of
demagogy and demagogic practices that go too far.

Seventh, the character of campaign discussion reflects the
limitations, capacities, and conventions of the media of communication. The media, as has been shown in previous chapters, can exert a great deal of influence on campaign practices
by the manner in which they report them. The economics of
mass communication, involving as it does high costs of access
and relatively low distribution costs, sets limits on the number
who can effectively enter competition for public support and
increases the influence of those who can. The technical capacities of the media determine their content in part. If television has made personality appeals more important in campaigns, it is not because politicians have not always had the
motives to make such appeals, but because television is such
an incomparable instrument to convey them.

Eighth, the expectations of the electorate as to the forms
campaign discussion will take are a determinant of the forms
it does take. At any given time a set of practices will be accepted as the kind of thing that goes on in campaigns, and,
whether or not members of the public consider such practices
as "good," their tolerance will encourage campaigners to continue them. If, for example, the public expects campaigners
to launch personal attacks on each other, they are quite likely
to do so whenever it suits their interests. Over time, public
expectations and the customs of campaigning change slowly
and together. Forms of vilification that were taken as a matter
of course in the early years of the nation's political life would
now be thought both exceptional and in bad taste. In the early

nineteenth century politicians feared public disapproval of any electioneering they might do on their own behalf; now they are more likely to fear public criticism for aloofness if they fail to campaign in person. Face-to-face debates seem at one time to have been a normal and expected form of campaigning, particularly in the Southern states; they are now relatively infrequent.[6]

Ninth, the legal framework within which campaign discussion is carried on shapes its form and content. The significance of law as an influence on campaigns may be easily overlooked because the number of laws that campaigners must take into account is relatively small and many of those formally regulating campaign practices are without real effect. Some laws, however—Section 315 of the Federal Communications Act would be a good example—do have quite real consequences for campaigning. Moreover, the lack of some possible legal controls may be considered a fact of importance in explaining why American campaigning assumes the forms it does.

[6] A veteran Southern politician, discussing the demise of the debate in 1889, had this to say: "Forty years ago, constant practice had made our public speakers so skillful in debate that every question was made clear even to men otherwise uneducated. For the last twenty years this practical union between politicians and people has not existed. Only one party is allowed to speak, and the leaders of that party no longer debate, they simply declaim and denounce. Upon this crude and windy diet, the once robust and sturdy political convictions of our people have dwindled into leanness and decay. In my judgment, this state of affairs is fatally injurious to our institutions, and dangerous to our liberties. The people follow with confidence the misleading and uncontradicted assertions of their leaders, and act upon false impressions, to their own prejudice and the injury of the common good. The evil of mischievous assertion is greatly lessened when free discussion is allowed, and error exposed and combated by the unsparing vigor of an opposing party. Free government becomes an absurdity when all shades of opinion are not allowed the fullest expression." (Reuben Davis, *Recollections of Mississippi and Mississippians,* 1889, pp. 195-96.) Rule 18 of the Democratic Party of South Carolina seems to be a vestige of the custom of holding debates between candidates. It provides that the State Committee shall arrange joint meetings of candidates for the same offices in different localities, although no candidate is compelled to participate. Rules of the Democratic Party of South Carolina, 1952-54, adopted by the Democratic State Convention, April 19, 1950.

Tenth, the relationship of campaigners to each other and to the campaign audience shapes the strategy of campaigners and hence the content of campaign communication. When the attention of the campaign audience is discontinuous and segmented, campaigners will tend to sloganize their appeals; there will be a great deal of repetition; and ambiguity, evasion of issues, distortion, and irrelevance will be encouraged. When rival candidates address an identical audience that gives them continuing attention, they will be encouraged to clarify their respective positions, they will hesitate to give distorted accounts of events or of their opponents' positions, and campaign discussion will tend to assume a challenge-and-response form. When campaign discussion takes a dialogue form, as in the press conference or the forum, the ambiguity of appeals is reduced; when it assumes a monologue form, as in the typical campaign speech, appeals become more ambiguous. When it is difficult for the campaign audience to establish the identity, character, and interests of those sponsoring campaign communication, campaign discussion will be characterized by a greater number of distortions, falsehoods, and appeals to politically divisive prejudices. When the reverse is true, these will be less prominent features of campaign communications.

While there is little that is novel in this listing of the factors that determine the character of campaign communication, students of campaigning have too often written as though one or another of them could alone explain what goes on in campaigns. They have, in fact, tended to emphasize the importance of those that are, in the short run, least subject to change—the party and electoral system, the competitive character of campaign communication, and the character and quality of the electorate. The distinguishing feature of the analysis that has been presented here has been its insistence that there is no one-to-one relationship between the quality of campaign discussion and any single factor, and that some of those that have a considerable influence on the character of campaign discussion have received less attention than they deserve. What campaigners do is the product of a great many different influences, some that remain constant over long periods of time, some less enduring and more amenable to conscious control. Few would want to change the constitutional status of speech and publication. The party and electoral systems, the competitive nature of campaign discussion, and the character of the electorate and of campaigners are relatively insusceptible to change or change slowly. The financing of communication, the expectations of the electorate, the legal framework of campaign communication, and the character of the audience-candidate relationship, however, are factors that are more easily acted on.

This conclusion suggests a strategy, the elements of which have been previously considered, for those who would seek to increase the contribution that campaign discussion can make to the rationality of electoral decisions. They should seek to encourage the distribution of all information relevant to the voters' decision, to ensure some equality in access to the electorate for rival candidates; to encourage those forms of campaigning that establish a relationship between audience and candidates similar to that presupposed by debate; to make campaign discussion less a monologue of propagandist to electorate and more a dialogue between them; to build a public demand for those forms of campaigning that lend most encouragement to rational discourse; and, where possible, given the constitutional status of speech and publication, to penalize campaigners who engage in practices that subvert the ability of voters to choose rationally.

Legislators could contribute to the success of such a strategy both by facilitating competition in campaign communication on more equal terms and by penalizing undesirable practices. They could revise Section 315 of the Federal Communications

Act, limiting its application to major party candidates. They could subsidize certain forms of campaign communication—particularly voters' pamphlets and radio and television joint encounters—and thus encourage, if not require, their use. They could extend the franking privilege to candidates. They could withdraw the conditional privilege from false statements about candidates and enact measures to penalize false statements and last minute attacks. They could make anti-smear legislation enforceable by injunctions, by civil suits to void elections, and by citizen initiated election inquests. They could grant candidates the right of reply, require campaign organizations to get their candidate's approval for campaign literature, and require the sponsors of campaign communication to disclose more adequately their interests and identity.

The press, too, could do a great deal to alter the character of the campaign, if publishers and editors were to accept that as an objective. Simple reporting of the newsworthy statements of campaigners, without comment or without additional factual background, is not enough. There needs to be a greater effort on the part of the press to present the statements of candidates and other partisans in the context of their own past records and statements and of those of their opponents. Such reporting would do something to discourage the more flagrant distortions in campaign discussion. Editors should not hesitate to refuse to print charges made at such times and in such a manner as to foreclose the possibility of adequate reply. They could usefully give fuller reports of some aspects of the campaign—particularly of the activities and character of non-party campaign organizations. They could insist on regular press conferences as an integral part of the campaign. They could experiment with various forms of the battle pages. They could help voters to compare the records, positions, and promises of candidates in issue-by-issue campaign feature stories.

Citizen group action, finally, could do much to increase the contributions of campaign discussion to rational electoral decisions. The most fundamental task such groups could assume would be to clarify the social functions of campaigning and to build a public demand for the kind of campaigning that would serve those functions well. They could build a demand for those forms of campaigning that make debate and cross examination possible and seek to enforce such demands on campaigners. They could make efforts to secure legislation that would facilitate campaign discussion and penalize undesirable practices. They could press for the enforcement of such legislation and of existing laws. They could sponsor forums, debates, and press conferences. Citizen group action and legislation would depend on each other for success: The latter is unlikely to be either passed or enforced without the support of citizen groups, and citizen groups will hardly be able to realize their full potential in reshaping campaigning without supporting legislation.

From where might the impetus for such action come? It is unlikely to come from the public as a whole—the issues are too subtle, the capacity of the public for organized action too small. It might come, in the proper circumstances, from parties and politicians, for, in almost every conflict situation, it is in the interest of one or the other of the participants to change the rules. It might come, too, from members of what has been termed the quality electorate. Capable of appreciating the importance of policy differences and differing qualifications in candidates, they are those most severely deprived by a campaign discussion that consists of a pummeling of stuffed figures. They are also in a position to make their influence felt in citizen groups, in the press, and in legislatures.

Index

Almond, Gabriel A., 151n
Anonymous propaganda
  campaign organizations, similarity
    to fronts, 133-36
  control of, 136-45
    enforcement of laws, 138-39
    limitations of laws, 136-38
    revision of laws, 140-45
  forms of, 129
  front organizations, 131-34
  influence on electorate, 130-36
    passim
  by party committees, 134

Baus, Herbert, 42n
Baxter, Leone, 41, 42n, 78, 78n
Benson, Ezra Taft, 64-65
Berdahl, Clarence, 46n
Berelson, Bernard, 27n, 28, 29, 30, 61
Bone, Hugh, 46n, 129, 130n, 134n
British election laws, 39, 120, 123
Bryce, James, 25n, 61, 90
Butler, Paul M., 110n, 111-12

Campaign discussion
  changing the character of, 75-83
  distortion in, 51-58 passim, 59-60,
    63-64
  factors, review of, 148-55
  free discussion and integrity of
    elections, 101-4
  inevitability of shortcomings, 16-17
  purposes of, 8-9
  variations through different media,
    72-75
Campaign literature. See also Anonymous propaganda

by League of Women Voters, 81
  patterns of discussion in, 74
  voters' pamphlets, 37-38, 41-42, 80
Campaigns, types of, 5
Candidates
  determining "leading," 44
  personal attacks on, 85-126. See also
    Defamation
    curbing by press and public, 106-
      13, 124
    curbing through legal revisions,
      113-19
    enforcement of legal provisions,
      119-24
    libel suits, 98-100
    methods to control, 101-4
    responses to, 90-93
    right of reply, 117-19
    timing of, 89
  protecting against anonymous at-
    tack, 127-45. See also Anonymous
    propaganda
Carroll, Wallace, 76, 79
Chotiner, Murray, 78n
Citizen groups, 81-83, 106, 108-13,
  124, 156-57. See also Committee of
  Seventy; Fair Campaign Practices
  Committee: League of Women
  Voters
Classical theories of free speech, 11-
  12. See also Mill, John Stuart
Committee of Seventy, 108-9, 112-13
Communications Act, Federal. See
  Communications Act, Federal, un-
  der Legislation
Congressional privilege, 96-98, 115
Corrupt Practices Act, Federal. See